FREEDOM AND FATE

An Inner Life of
RALPH WALDO EMERSON

STEPHEN E. WHICHER

Philadelphia

UNIVERSITY OF PENNSYLVANIA PRESS

1953

Published in Great Britain, India, and Pakistan
by Geoffrey Cumberlege: Oxford University Press
London, Bombay, and Karachi

To

My Mother

and

My Father

Preface

EMERSON enjoyed, as he wished, an original relation to the universe, one which, like all living relationships, developed and altered with time. Throughout his life he followed the advice of the poet who speaks at the end of *Nature:* 'Build therefore your own world.' His different insights are so many rays of organization thrown out by the exploring soul, in the words of Bacon he cited so often, to conform the shows of things to the desires of the mind.

As his mind was complex and many-sided, so was the world it built. His greatest gift was his ability to endure the push and pull of contrary directions in his thought without a premature reaching out after conclusions that would do violence to his whole nature. Typically, he came to terms with conflicts as they developed among his truths by dramatizing them, by giving their opposition full play on the stage of his work. Consequently, his writings, and particularly his journals, record a genuine drama of ideas, a still little-known story that adds a new dimension of interest to his thought. This book is intended to 'produce' that drama. It traces Emerson's surprisingly eventful voyage in the world of the mind.

Perhaps one should define more particularly the relation of this book to the recent *Life of Ralph Waldo Emerson* by Ralph L. Rusk, since that is in so many ways definitive. There is obviously no comparison in scope or achievement. Professor Rusk's monument of thorough and discerning scholarship is the best portrait we can hope to have of the life Emerson's contemporaries witnessed; it does not attempt, however, to take us very far into the life of his mind. Yet few men, few writers even, have lived more entirely in the mind than he. I offer a complementary sketch of the inner life of Ralph Waldo Emerson, the life—so much more real to him—of which the only record is his works.

My short interpretation of his message has been a long time growing. At one time or another I have read virtually everything that has been written about Emerson, but my many debts to specific works are mostly now irrecoverable. I have tried to list in my bibliography all that have helped me. A few, however, should be mentioned here.

Of previous studies of Emerson's thought, I have learned most from the monograph of Henry David Gray.* His statement of the general philosophic problem Emerson faced as a nineteenth-century idealist, and of the successive answers he appeared to give to it, is still indispensable. Gray's work was completed, however, almost fifty years ago, before the journals were published, and needs restatement in the light of later scholarship; his intention, also, was more theoretic and systematic than mine. Henry Nash Smith's article on 'Emerson's Problem of Vocation' suggested to me the whole conception of a drama in Emerson's ideas. It comes to grips with an important problem in his thought in a way that has been a model to me of the method I wished to use. Joseph Warren Beach's study of Emerson and evolution seems to me definitive, and his examination of Emerson's nature poetry is repeatedly rewarding. I have depended on it heavily in my eighth chapter.

F. O. Matthiessen's *American Renaissance* includes the most minute and sensitive examination ever given to the character of Emerson's mind. Matthiessen carefully, perhaps too carefully, confines his attention to Emerson's immediate esthetic experience and avoids discussion of his thought except as it affects the character of his art. Even so, no study of Emerson's mind can be without an extensive debt to his work. Finally, my understanding of Emerson's Puritan background, the most important single fact about him, derives primarily from the works of Perry Miller, notably his article 'Jonathan Edwards to Emerson,' and from the first two papers in Henry Bamford Parkes's *The Pragmatic Test*, a treatment of the subject which deserves to be much better known than it is.

Really?

((

* The full form of all short references may be found in the Bibliography, in which they are listed alphabetically by author.

Every student of Emerson, of course, must depend at countless points on two encyclopedias of Emerson information, Ralph L. Rusk's edition of Emerson's letters, and Kenneth Walter Cameron's *Emerson the Essayist*. As this is written I have not seen the recent study of Emerson's thought by Sherman Paul. I regret that Vivian C. Hopkins' *Spires of Form* appeared too late for me to use as I would have wished.

This book is in a very real sense one more of the many contributions to scholarship in American literature by Professor Robert E. Spiller, without whose incisive criticism and generous practical help in seeing the manuscript through the press it would have been a poorer and later volume. (I alone am to be blamed for its faults.) It began as a thesis under the direction of Professor Perry Miller and owes a great debt to his imaginative teaching and impressive synthesizing power. For their assistance at various stages of this study I am much indebted also to Professors George J. Becker, Gail Kennedy, Arthur O. Lovejoy, Ralph Barton Perry, the late Theodore Spencer, and in particular to Professor Frederick I. Carpenter.

Mr. Phelps Soule and the University of Pennsylvania Press have handled a fussy task with admirable tact and skill. Mr. William A. Jackson and Miss Carolyn Jakeman of the Houghton Library in Cambridge were unfailingly helpful. My book could not have been written without the aid of a 'Post-War' Fellowship from the Rockefeller Foundation in 1946-47. As for what I owe my parents, Professor and Mrs. George F. Whicher, and my wife, Elizabeth Trickey Whicher—such debts are beyond statement.

I am particularly grateful to Professor Edward Waldo Forbes and the Emerson Memorial Association for permission to see and use some of Emerson's unpublished lectures, and to quote from his sermons, journals, works, and letters; and to the Houghton Mifflin Company for their permission to quote from *The Journals of Ralph Waldo Emerson* (1909-14), from his *Complete Works* (Centenary Edition, 1903-4), and from Arthur C. McGiffert, Jr., *Young Emerson Speaks* (1938). I acknowledge further permissions to quote as follows: Ralph L.

Rusk and Charles Scribner's Sons, for permission to quote from *The Life of Ralph Waldo Emerson,* by Ralph L. Rusk (1949); Ralph L. Rusk and the Columbia University Press, for *The Letters of Ralph Waldo Emerson,* ed. Ralph L. Rusk (1939); the Columbia University Press, for *A History of American Philosophy,* by Herbert W. Schneider (1946); the Macmillan Company, for *The Concept of Nature in Nineteenth-Century English Poetry,* by Joseph Warren Beach (1936), and *The New England Mind: The Seventeenth Century,* by Perry Miller (1939); the Oxford University Press, for *American Renaissance,* by F. O. Matthiessen (1941); Harcourt, Brace and Company, for *Four Quartets,* by T. S. Eliot (1943); New Directions, for *Maule's Curse,* by Yvor Winters (1938); Frederick I. Carpenter and the Harvard University Press, for *Emerson and Asia,* by Professor Carpenter (1930); the *New England Quarterly* and Merrell R. Davis, for his article 'Emerson's "Reason" and the Scottish Philosophers' (June 1944); and Kenneth Walter Cameron for his *Emerson the Essayist* (1945).

S. E. W.

Oslo, Norway
May 1953

Contents

The Outer Life (Chronology)

1803 (May 25) Born at Boston, Massachusetts.
1811 (May 12) Death of father, William Emerson.
1817 (September) Admitted to Harvard College.
1821 (August) Graduated from Harvard College.
1818-26 Schoolteaching.
1825 (February) Admitted to Harvard Divinity School.
  Brother William returned from Germany, renounced ministry.
1826 Read *Observations on the Growth of the Mind*, by Sampson Reed (Swedenborgian classmate).
  First read Coleridge.
  (October 10) Approbated to preach.
1826-27 (November-May) Traveled in South.
1827 (March) Met Achille Murat.
1828 Temporary insanity of brother Edward.
1829 (March 11) Ordination at Second Church, Boston.
  (September 30) Married to Ellen Tucker.
1829-31 Renewed reading in Coleridge.
1830 Edward to West Indies for health.
1831 (February 8) Death of Ellen.
1832 (October 28) Resignation from Second Church accepted.
1832-33 (December 25-October 7) Traveled in Europe.
1833 (August 25) Met Carlyle.
1833-34 Early lectures on natural history.
1834 (October) Moved to Concord.
  (October 10) Death of Edward.
1835 Lectures on *Biography:* 'Tests of Great Men' (?) (Jan. 29); 'Michelangelo' (Feb. 5); 'Martin Luther' (Feb. 12); 'John Milton' (Feb. 20); 'George Fox' (Feb. 26); 'Edmund Burke' (Mar. 5).
  Met Alcott.
  (August 20) Lecture on 'The Best Mode of Inspiring a Correct Taste in English Literature.'
  (September 14) Married Lydia Jackson.
1835-36 (November 5-January 14) Lectures on *English Literature.*

1836   Met Thoreau (?).
        (May 9) Death of brother Charles.
        (September 9) Publication of *Nature*.
        (September 19) First meeting of the 'Transcendental
        Club.'
        (October 30) Birth of Waldo.

1836-37 Lectures on *The Philosophy of History:* 'Introductory'
        (Dec. 8, 15); 'Humanity of Science' (Dec. 22); 'Art'
        (Dec. 29); 'Literature' (Jan. 5); 'Politics' (Jan. 12);
        'Religion' (Jan. 19); 'Society' (Jan. 26); 'Trades and
        Professions' (Feb. 2); 'Manners' (Feb. 9); 'Ethics'
        (Feb. 16); 'The Present Age' (Feb. 23); '[Individual-
        ism]' (Mar. 2).

1837   (June 10) Address on education at the Greene St. School,
        Providence, R. I.
        (August 31) *The American Scholar:* An Oration Deliv-
        ered Before the Phi Beta Kappa Society, at Cambridge.

1837-38 Lectures on *Human Culture:* 'Introductory' (Dec. 6);
        'Doctrine of the Hands' (Dec. 13); 'The Head' (Dec.
        20); 'Eye and Ear' (Dec. 27); 'The Heart' (Jan. 3);
        'Being and Seeming' (Jan. 10); 'Prudence' (Jan. 17);
        'Heroism' (Jan. 24); 'Holiness' (Jan. 31); 'General
        Views' (Feb 7).

1838   (July 15) *An Address:* Delivered Before the Senior Class
        in Divinity College, Cambridge.
        (July 24) Oration on 'Literary Ethics.'

1838-39 Lectures on *Human Life:* 'The Doctrine of the Soul' (Dec.
        5); 'Home' (Dec. 12); 'The School' (Dec. 19);
        'Love' (Dec. 26); 'Genius' (Jan. 9); 'The Protest'
        (Jan. 16); 'Tragedy' (Jan. 23); 'Comedy' (Jan. 30);
        'Duty' (Feb. 6); 'Demonology' (Feb. 20).

1839   (February 24) Birth of Ellen.

1839-40 Lectures on *The Present Age:* 'Introduction' (Dec. 4);
        'Literature' (1) (Dec. 11); 'Literature' (2) (Dec. 18);
        'Politics' (Jan. 1); 'Private Life' (Jan. 8); 'Reforms'
        (Jan. 15); 'Religion' (Jan. 22); 'Ethics' (Jan. 29);
        'Education' (Feb. 5); 'Tendencies' (Feb. 12).

1841   (January 25) Lecture on 'Man the Reformer.'
        (March 20) *Essays, First Series,* published: 'History,'
        'Self-Reliance,' 'Compensation,' 'Spiritual Laws,' 'Love,'

'Friendship,' 'Prudence,' 'Heroism,' 'The Over-Soul,'
'Circles,' 'Intellect,' 'Art.'
(August 11) Lecture on 'The Method of Nature.'
(November 22) Birth of Edith.

1841-42   Lectures on *The Times:* 'Introduction' (Dec. 2); 'The
Conservative' (Dec. 9); 'The Poet' (Dec. 16); 'The
Transcendentalist' (Dec. 23); 'Manners' (Dec. 30);
'Character' (Jan. 6); 'Relation of Man to Nature' (Jan.
13); 'Prospects' (Jan. 20).

1842   (January 27) Death of Waldo.

1844   (July 10) Birth of Edward.
(October 19) *Essays, Second Series,* published: 'The Poet,'
'Experience,' 'Character,' 'Manners,' 'Gifts,' 'Nature,'
'Politics,' 'Nominalist and Realist,' 'New England Re-
formers.'

1845-46   Lectures on *Representative Men:* 'The Uses of Great Men'
(Dec. 11); 'Plato, [or] the Philosopher' (Dec. 18);
'Swedenborg, or the Mystic' (Dec. 25); 'Montaigne, or
the Skeptic' (Jan. 1); 'Napoleon, or the Man of the
World' (Jan. 8); 'Shakespeare, or the Poet' (Jan. 15);
'Goethe, or the Writer' (Jan. 22).

1846   (December 25) *Poems* published.

1847-48   (October 5-July 27) Second trip to England and Europe.

1849   (September) *Nature; Addresses and Lectures* published.
(December) *Representative Men* published.

1851   Lectures on *The Conduct of Life* at Pittsburgh: 'Introductory: Laws of Success' (Mar. 22); 'Wealth' (Mar.
25); 'Economy' (Mar. 27); 'Culture' (Mar. 29);
'Power' (not given); 'Worship' (Apr. 1).

1856   (August 6) *English Traits* published.

1860   (December 8) *The Conduct of Life* published: 'Fate,'
'Power,' 'Wealth,' 'Culture,' 'Behavior,' 'Worship,'
'Considerations by the Way,' 'Beauty,' 'Illusions.'

1867   (April 28) *May-Day and Other Pieces* published.

1870   (March) *Society and Solitude* published.

1872   (July 24) Burning of house.

1872-73   (October 23-May 27) Third trip to Europe.

1875   Beginning of Cabot's aid with manuscripts.

1882   (April 27) Death at Concord, Massachusetts.

NOTE: The body of this book focuses on the fourteen years between Emerson's first and second journeys to Europe, 1833-47, his intellectual prime, though the first chapter brings him up to this point and the last two take him beyond it. The remaining chapters divide this period roughly between them, the first four dealing with his early challenge, the next three with his subsequent acquiescence. The dividing line between these two subperiods is hopelessly inexact, since he passed through an extended time of relative trouble and uncertainty as his thought adjusted itself to a complex of new influences. Perhaps a table, vague as it must be, will be of use:

1803-32	Unitarian period
1830-32	First crisis
1832-41	Period of challenge
(1838-44)	(Second crisis)
1841-82	Period of acquiescence

PART I

FREEDOM

CHAPTER ONE

Discovery

EMERSON came late into his force. The years recorded in the first two volumes of his journal—those before his resignation from the Second Church—show little distinction of style or thought. If he had died before the age of thirty-three, as he more than once feared he might, no one would have guessed the country's loss. Such slow development, of course, has been the rule among major American writers; Whitman, Melville, Hawthorne, Thoreau, to name only those of Emerson's time, published little of importance before middle life. In Emerson's case, the surprising thing is that he ever reached greatness at all. The most serious and seemingly permanent disabilities inhibited his strength as a young man. It took something like a spiritual miracle, as glorious as it was unforeseen, to release his latent powers.

To begin with, there was his poor health. A tubercular, like many in his family—two brothers eventually died of the disease—he was engaged throughout his twenties in a serious battle of life and death in which he was not at all sure of winning. The grim winter of 1826-27, in particular, he spent in exile in the South, watching his health and strength ebb from him, half-doubting that he would see his home again. Zealously ambitious to shine as a writer and preacher, he was forced throughout this time, on pain of death, to 'lounge,' undertaking little, waiting for the slow well of his vitality to refill. Though his health improved in later life, and he developed, indeed, unusual endurance and capacity for work, robust vigor like Whitman's was never his; he thought of himself always, like Henry Adams, as condemned by nature to be a spectator of life.

With this low vitality went a crippling self-distrust. As the slender young man compared himself with his ambitions, he felt

3

a disheartening sense of incapacity. He was incurably idle and
self-indulgent, he imagined, given to 'intellectual dissipation'—
that is, he read what caught his eye instead of what he thought
was good for him—constrained and uneasy in the company
of others, cold and unresponsive in his affections. Admiring pur-
poseful scholarship and consecutive reasoning, practical skill and
personal forcefulness, all of which, he was convinced, were the
only means to the preëminence he aspired to, he found himself
sadly deficient in them all and alternated between a strained
self-exhortation and rueful resignation. Though his early journals often show a manly courage and good sense, the dominant
mood is a sense of impotence. He has no strength to shape his
own destiny and feels himself drifting, sometimes in humilia-
tion, sometimes in stoic amusement, before the inexorable flight
of time. 'We put up with Time and Chance because it costs
too great an effort to subdue them to our wills, and minds that
feel an embryo greatness stirring within them let it die for want
of nourishment. Plans that only want maturity, ideas that only
need explanation to lead the thinker on to a far nobler being
than now he dreams of . . . are suffered to languish and blight
in hopeless barrenness.'[1]

The note of regret at his hopeless barrenness which emerges
in his journal before he is yet twenty is, of course, largely unjus-
tified, the mingled product of the depression resulting from his
poor health and the unreasonableness of his hopes. Ambition
was a killer with the Emersons; both Charles and Edward fell
before its lash. Ralph also was an idolator of glory and habitually searched his character for signs of greatness. Yet his refusal,
against the nagging of a tyrannous conscience, to push himself
beyond his strength, undoubtedly saved his life. What he gained
in longevity he lost in self-esteem.

His early ambition shook his confidence not only by its
Puritanical extremism, but by its false direction. In his well-
known self-examination at the age of twenty-one he solemnly
dedicates himself to the Church. '. . . in Divinity I hope to

[1] References and dates for quotations may be found by looking under the
page on which the quotation *begins,* among the References.

thrive. I inherit from my sire . . . a passionate love for the strains of eloquence. I burn after the *"aliquid immensum infinitumque"* which Cicero desired. . . . In my better hours, I am the believer (if not the dupe) of brilliant promises, and can respect myself as the possessor of those powers which command the reason and passions of the multitude. The office of a clergyman is twofold: public preaching and private influence. Entire success in the first is the lot of few, but this I am encouraged to expect. If, however, the individual himself lack that moral worth which is to secure the last, his studies upon the first are idly spent. . . . My trust is that my profession shall be my regeneration of mind, manners, inward and outward estate; or rather my starting-point, for I have hoped to put on eloquence as a robe, and by goodness and zeal and the awfulness of Virtue to press and prevail over the false judgments, the rebel passions and corrupt habits of men.'

It is not hard to see that what is genuine in this declaration is literary. The clergy had always been the literary class in New England—his father was a good example of the breed—and the young man dreams of following in this path. The unlikely moral reformation of others and of himself to which his choice commits him is by comparison, while also sincere, an imposed goal, a burden of duty that he does not really welcome. As for the patient labor in the vineyard that is most of a preacher's vocation, he hardly seems aware of this part of the contract; as he became so, the vigor of his recoil showed its foreignness to his independent nature. As long as he was committed to the attempt to put on a professional character 'as a robe,' rather than to realize his own, he was likely to continue to feel and show a 'want of sufficient *bottom* in my nature.'

The development of Emerson's powers was held back most of all, however, by his battle with scepticism. In the young Emerson we have a 'natural believer' who has not yet found an adequate faith. During the 1820's he himself felt the threat of what he later described as the disease of the age, Unbelief, and with it of the paralyzing 'Uncertainty as to what we ought to do.' We cannot understand the zeal with which a pious and

seemingly conservative young man later plunged into a career
of radical heresy without appreciating this obscure emergency
in his early thought. Though the insight that released him
seemed to him, when it came at last, an 'amazing revelation,'
its growth as we trace it in the record has a quality of inevitability. Everything united to bring him to it: his personal and
temperamental needs, his lack of genuine calling to the regular
ministry, the inherent logic of the sceptical crisis in the Unitarianism of his youth, the heady doctrines of 'modern philosophy' just then seeping into New England from their fountain-
head in Germany, his Calvinist-bred need for a religion of the
heart, a need which Unitarianism had neither eradicated nor satisfied. The new faith, like a snake's skin, grew beneath the old,
until, when the moment came, the old husk was cast off.

The story of its growth begins with a provincial New England
Unitarian, to all appearances a creditable and typical product
of early nineteenth-century Harvard. If Dr. William Ellery
Channing, the leading spokesman of Unitarianism and the
young man's model for eloquence, or his Harvard teachers,
could have read his letters and journals, they would have found
little not to approbate. He is the declared champion of the
benevolent, moralistic faith in which he had been indoctrinated.
Yet Unitarian Christianity was already far gone in 'Infidelity.'
During Emerson's college years, Channing's Baltimore sermon
openly confirmed a rift between the liberal Christianity of the
Boston area and the conservative Calvinism of the hinterland
that had been growing for a generation. The central difference
was the Unitarian denial of the 'ruined state of man.' Retaining
the Puritan zeal for righteousness, the Unitarians rejected the
Puritan doctrine of man's innate depravity—a doctrine already
craftily qualified by many professed Calvinists—and flatly asserted man's free moral agency. The result was to complete the
slow drift of Boston from the God-centered piety of the Puritans
to a man-centered religion of duty. God was no longer a searing

flame of power, before whose unsearchable will man must bow in awe and love; He was a benevolent Father who designed and governed the world to assist man in his moral education. Christ came to teach man virtue by his example; holiness consisted in moral perfection.

Essentially, Boston Unitarianism represents the marriage of New England Puritanism and the Enlightenment—the farthest, perhaps, that the Puritan mind could go to meet the Age of Reason without, like Franklin, leaving its Puritanism behind altogether. If, from one point of view, it grows by an imperceptible transition from Puritanism and retains a Puritan character, from another it takes a stand toward Calvinism like that of the eighteenth-century philosophers toward medieval superstition. It also protests against the 'degrading errors' of an outworn theology in the name of reason; and like them also it identifies the rational with a really dogmatic humanitarian gospel. No friends of merely natural religion, Unitarians continued to accept the external authority of scriptural revelation as the ground for their faith. But they insisted that 'Christianity is a rational religion.' Scripture must be interpreted by reason and could contain nothing not consonant with the laws of nature. Yet in point of fact their ultimate test of religious truth was not reason but their sense of right. The real law they recognized was the moral code of their society. Thus the grounds of Unitarian faith, in theory one, were actually three: revelation, the formal ground; reason, the theoretical test of revelation; and moral sense, the actual test of reason.

But the identity of right and reason was a more difficult and uneasy assumption in nineteenth-century Boston than in eighteenth-century London or Paris. Reason had shown itself a double-edged weapon, capable not only of lopping off superstitions but also of striking at the root of religious faith. Deism, scepticism, French materialism and atheism, and latterly the higher criticism of the Germans, all amply demonstrated the havoc that unchecked reason could make of religion. Unitarians were thus forced to steer between the Scylla of enthusiasm and

the Charybdis of scepticism. The nice seamanship required must
have had much to do with the cautious chill of their supposedly
plain and simple faith.

Emerson's position in the 1820's, as the first-generation
product of this situation, may be characterized by saying that
he found the channel converging ahead of him and became sensible that he was heading for the rocks. Of the three grounds
of Unitarian belief—revelation, reason, and moral sense—both
revelation and reason lost authority with him, and only 'the fine
clue of moral perception' was left to lead him out of the labyrinth of his doubts. His difficulties with rational religion had two
chief sources: the doubtful authority on which this faith rested,
and the responsibility for an unceasing effort at self-culture that
it placed on his individual powers.

While, in the revealing self-examination already quoted, he
claims a strong imagination and a passionate love for the strains
of eloquence and bases his hope to thrive as a preacher on these
qualities, he finds at the same time, 'My reasoning faculty is
proportionably weak. . . .' His thought did not take kindly to
trains of reasoned argument but followed an unpredictable ebb
and flow. 'Whether any laws fix them, and what the laws are,
I cannot ascertain.' Even the glooms and glories of the ancestral
Calvinism were more congenial to such a temperament than
'reason, cool as cucumber.' We find many reminders in the
early journals that his star rained on him influences of ancestral
religion and taught him of a vanished depth of the religious
sentiment unknown at Cambridge. Certainly this was the direction of the influence of his Aunt Mary Moody Emerson, the
Weird-woman of her religion, to whom he constantly confessed
his doubts and problems in the 1820's, and who showed him
in her conversation and letters something of the white-hot core
of the original Calvinistic piety. At the same time her fierce
ambition nourished his brilliant visions of future grandeur and
whetted his desire to shine. The ideal of cool reason presented
to him at Cambridge found little to build on here and operated
only to intensify his self-distrust.

Most deeply, his personal experience did not confirm the Unitarian claims for human freedom. His periods of mentality were not under his control but were 'determined by something out of me and higher than me.' If he was ever to know the freedom the Unitarians too complacently assured him was his, or the greatness he aspired to reach, he would first have to throw off their paralyzing assumption that he could win them through the exercise of his own individual powers. Experience showed him the hollowness of this claim and for a while threw him back on the old formulas of humility. 'We are such bubbles that when we mount, we see not how; and when we grow great, we cannot commend ourselves.'

During the same period Emerson was much exercised in his mind to find an answer to the queries of the sceptic. The sceptic without doubt was wrong; but it was not enough to say so—he must be refuted on his own ground by rational argument. Given his dialectical skill, and the vulnerability of rational religion to rational attack, this was no light task. Emerson's attitude to the problem is a characteristic mixture of open-minded curiosity and impervious dogmatism, alarm and complacency. In these years, however, his security was weaker and his concern greater than they ever became again. Reading his journals of the time, we watch a balked, hovering affirmation, searching for a safe landing-place. Though some of the speculative flights of his later life took him fairly far from home, he never again showed the same lack of orientation.

The 'sceptic,' as he used the name in the 1820's, was primarily the man who questioned natural and revealed religion. Classical scepticism and pyrrhonism, Montaigne, and the double-edged 'Berkleian philosophy' provided subordinate connotations; when he later wrote an essay on 'Montaigne: or, The Skeptic' they had worked to the forefront, and he spelt the name with a 'k' in recognition of the shift. Now, the sceptic was one who disbelieved in God, immortality, and the truth of Christianity. Though his mental image of the sceptic was compounded from various sources, most of them indirect—one might mention, beyond those listed above, Gibbon, Voltaire, 'the Germans,' and above all his personal acquaintance with the French atheist, Achille Murat—its features bore an unmistakable resemblance to the Scotch Goliath, David Hume. The repeated mentions of this greatest of contemporary sceptics in Emerson's early letters and journals are a convenient clue to the struggle with scepticism which was then dampening his faith.

His Bowdoin Prize Dissertation of 1821, 'The Present State of Ethical Philosophy,' written in his senior year in college, indicates that he had already learned to respect the formidable doubts raised by Hume, and even to suspect that he did not have his match among the orthodox. From then to 1829 at least, Emerson repeatedly read in Hume, remarked on him in his journal, and discussed him in letters to his friends. He was most garrulous about Hume and scepticism in some early letters to his aunt. In 1823, for example, asserting, 'Every day . . . I ramble among doubts to which my reason offers no solution,' he sent her a catalogue of curious questions which boil down pretty much to the one threadbare enigma, 'What is the Origin of Evil?' He had just been reading, or reading about, Hume's demonstration that 'events are conjoined, and not connected; that we have no knowledge but from experience. We have no experience of a Creator and there[fore] know of none,' and rallied his aunt with the name of 'this Deciever [sic].' 'Next comes the Scotch Goliath, David Hume; but . . . Who is he that can stand up before him & prove the existence of the Universe, & of its Founder? . . . Now though every one is daily referred to his own feelings as a triumphant confutation of the glozed lies of this Deceiver, yet, it assuredly would make us feel safer & prouder, to have our victorious answer set down in impregnable propositions.' A month later he plied her with more metaphysical difficulties, and the next year further half-jocular 'Humism' continued to arrive in Waterford and was recorded in his journal.

These sophomoric questionings, no doubt, spring chiefly from a desire to provoke a reply; they are the soul's mumps and measles and whooping cough. Nevertheless, time did not dissipate his doubts, as his continued concern with Hume and scepticism

shows; the problem was real. The trouble centered, for him and
for his Unitarian seniors, on the 'external evidences' of Christianity, the miracles by which Christ was held to have proved the
divine origin of his teachings. Emerson was alarmed at the
German higher criticism, for example, because their 'objections
. . . attack the foundations of external evidence, and so give up
the internal to historical speculators and pleasant doubters.' He
was aware that scepticism bore also on the belief in Providence
and a future state, and conceded on occasion that 'it is not certain
that God exists,' but he was incapable of taking such radical
denial seriously. After meeting Murat, he wrote in astonishment
to his brother, '. . . [he] is, yet, that which I had ever supposed
only a creature of the imagination—a consistent Atheist,—and a
disbeliever in the existence, and, of course, in the immortality
of the soul. My faith in these points is strong and I trust, as
I live, indestructible.'

   But the proofs of revelation were a different matter. Unitarians here had stumbled into an impasse. The belief that God
had once spoken to man, through his Son, and taught him the
way to salvation, was as necessary to Unitarians as to any other
variety of Christian then in New England. 'Reduce Christianity
to a set of abstract ideas,' Channing insisted, 'sever it from its
teacher, and it ceases to be the "power of God unto salvation." '
Yet the only visible evidence of Christ's divine authority, they
felt, was the Christian miracles; and here they ran head-on into
Hume, who had riddled the credibility of any reported miracle,
let alone such uncertain events of long ago as those retailed in
the New Testament. He demonstrated with what still seems
crushing finality that the idea of miracle had become an
anachronism in the Newtonian world of natural law. The Unitarians were thus forced into the position of insisting, as the only
rational proof of their faith, on a piece of irrational superstition,
and this visible contradiction caused them serious embarrass-
ment.

   In the 1820's, Emerson shared their belief that the preservation of his faith was bound up with Christianity as an institution,
and thus with the certainty of the Christian revelation. But the

implications of Hume's argument had now so sunk in that he could not, like the previous generation, really credit the Christian revelation, as attested by the Christian miracles. As a result, his faith was at Hume's mercy. Nothing better demonstrated this fact than the sermon on miracles which, as a Unitarian minister, he dutifully preached in 1831 to show his faith in them. The much erased manuscript bears the scars of the struggle it records between dogma and common sense. In the end the most he can manage to concede is that 'since I perceive the divine truth of the doctrine, I know the miracle must have been wrought which they say was wrought.' Clearly for Emerson the miracles have become a slightly discreditable and pointless adjunct to his faith, 'a lower species of evidence.' The opposite tendency, apparent in his journals, to follow the lead of Sampson Reed, the Swedenborgian druggist, and proclaim that 'All our life is a miracle' really represents a similar effort to get around the necessity of believing in any miracle in particular. His continued belief in the truth of Christianity rests to all practical purposes on internal evidence.

Yet he knew—certainly he was told so often enough—that internal evidence was sandy ground for faith. To 'enforce the burdensome doctrine of a Deity on the world,' as he once put it, you need 'State Reasons'; internal evidence can support only private conviction. His need to believe was thus left for a while without any sure basis and had to remain so until he could somehow find the means to vindicate internal evidence alone as a sufficient authority for faith. Meanwhile, he found himself face to face with what he once called 'the ghastly reality of things.' Eventually he found the means to strike through this ghastly mask to the living Reality beneath, and so escape the terrors of Unbelief. Yet the experience left its scar. Throughout his life, something in him stood aside from his own greatest flights of faith with a sceptical awareness that they were still but private dreams—mere sentiment and enthusiasm after all. When in later life he concerned himself again explicitly with 'skepticism,' he brought to the surface a deeply rooted strain of thought that had its origin in the same encounter with Unbelief in which his faith began.

The deepest legacy to him of this time of doubt and drifting was his lifelong recognition of necessity. The characteristic theme of the early journals is helplessness, a helplessness which his Stoicism and trust in Providence cannot finally disguise. His destiny seemed to work itself out with little help from him. 'I am the servant more than the master of my fates,' he wrote in 1824; and later, in the depths of his illness, 'I shape my fortunes, as it seems to me, not at all. For in all my life I obey a strong necessity. . . .' He felt himself the plaything of events and could meet their unpredictable succession with little more than a quizzical acquiescence. '—'T is a queer life, and the only humour proper to it seems quiet astonishment. Others laugh, weep, sell, or proselyte. I admire.'

Yet his early submission to necessity bred also a longing for freedom, all the more intense for his underlying sense of its impossibility. The force of his later transcendental faith, and its almost willful extravagance, sprang from his need to throw off, against all probability and common sense, his annihilating sense of dependence. The early record, perhaps, offers little promise of such escape. Beyond a barren self-respect, a Stoic obedience to duty, and a trust in the divine Providence that planned it that way, there seemed no means to mitigate his powerlessness. But beneath his surface passivity a deep revulsion against his servitude to a world he never made and did not accept was slowly gathering force, of which signs and portents are not lacking to those who examine the record after the event.

⟡

The way he would take was already clear in 1823: 'I see no reason why I should bow my head to man, or cringe in my demeanour. When the soul is disembodied, he that has nothing else but a towering independence has one claim to respect; whilst genius and learning may provoke our contempt for their supple knees. When I consider my poverty and ignorance, and the positive superiority of talents, virtues and manners, which I must acknowledge in many men, I am prone to merge my dignity in a most uncomfortable sense of unworthiness. But when I reflect that I am an immortal being, born to a destiny immeasurably high, deriving my moral and intellectual attributes directly from Almighty God, and that my existence and con-dition as his child must be forever independent of the controul and will of my fellow children,—I am elevated in my own eyes to a higher ground in life and a better self-esteem.' He offset his insignificance among men with the thought of his significance before God. In quest of independence and self-esteem, he swung from the world without to the world within.

He was helped by some elements in the intellectual system in which he was trained. There was, for example, the tradition of the 'moral sense.' This supposed human faculty, an innate, instinctive admiration for moral excellence at sight, was orig-inally advanced by Shaftesbury and Hutcheson as an answer to ethical thinkers of the time, like Hobbes, who traced all virtue to interest and advantage, and was transmitted to Emer-son from many sources, chief among which was the Scottish Realist, Dugald Stewart, whom he read in college and admired for several years afterwards. What this benevolent notion meant to Emerson was that conscience was not to be explained natural-istically. It was, as religion taught, the voice of God in the soul, teaching us an unquestionable law of conduct, testifying to the reality of a divine authority, and assuring us of the moral admin-istration of the universe. 'That sovereign sense,' then, was an early answer to scepticism. 'Dogmatists and philosophers,' he wrote in 1823, 'may easily convince me that my mind is but the abode of many passing shadows by the belief of whose existence about me I am mocked. . . . But it is in the constitution of the mind to rely with firmer confidence upon the *moral principle,* and I reject at once the idea of a delusion in this. . . . Upon the foundation of my *moral* sense I ground my faith in the immor-tality of the soul,' etc. If, as he now and then felt, 'our firmest faith in intellectual and moral truths sometimes passes away like the morning cloud before the queries of the sceptic,' yet an

impressive succession of British moralists assured him that an
escape from the puzzles to faith set by the sceptic was to be found
in 'the fine clue of moral perception.' Plentifully supplied as he
was with moral perceptions, this firsthand evidence of God,
morals, and immortality within his own mind did much to support his faith and self-esteem through their ebb in the twenties,
and easily enlarged, under later intellectual influences, into a
full belief in the God within us.[2]

A more ambiguous support came to him from the idealism
of Bishop Berkeley. It is improbable that Emerson ever read
much Berkeley; but 'the Berkleian philosophy,' better known
to Emerson as the 'Ideal Theory,' was a familiar topic of discussion in Stewart, since a major aim of Scotch Realism was to
challenge this line of thought.[3] Though Berkeley denied the
existence of a matter independent of perception in order to
confute sceptical materialism, as Stewart pointed out, to the
Realists the end-product of the Ideal Theory was the scepticism
of Hume. Berkeley questioned our knowledge of matter; Hume
also of mind: *all* we can know are 'impressions' and 'ideas.'
Emerson's first glimpse of the Berkeleian philosophy, then, if it
came through Stewart, was an unfavorable one, leading him to
lump together, as he did in his college dissertation, 'the visionary
schemes of Mr. Hume and Bishop Berkeley.' From then on,
however, he understood that, though 'I know that I exist,' we
do not know that there is any such thing as matter with the
same definitive certainty, and so this theory, like that of a
World Soul, could always be played with as a possibility, in a
scrap of verse, perhaps, or a spoofing letter to his brother. The
thought remained an ancient scepticism, allied on one side to
Pyrrho and on the other to Hume, more likely to shake than to
bolster belief.

Nevertheless, we may believe his later recollection, in a letter
to Margaret Fuller in 1841, of 'the joy with which in my boy-
hood I caught the first hint of the Berkleian philosophy, and
which I certainly never lost sight of afterwards.' He does

[2] See Appendix, Note A.
[3] See Appendix, Note B.

not mean, here or elsewhere, Berkeley's particular system, but simply the 'noble doubt . . . whether nature outwardly exists.' This seductive reversal of his relations to the world, with which the imagination of every child is sometime caught, transferring his recurrent sense of a dreaminess in his mode of life to outward nature, and releasing him in imagination into a solitude peopled with illusions, was scepticism of a special kind—illicit, no doubt, in that it vaporized the social world in which he was called to live and act, but still on occasion a needed if radical relief from the pressures of circumstances.

More important, he began to find that he could use this scepticism, as Berkeley used it, to fight scepticism. Thus he exorcised the name of Hume and all other free-thinkers of England and France, in a letter to his aunt in 1826, by an appeal to 'my old faith, that to each soul is a solitary law, a several universe. The colours to our eyes may be different, your red may be my green'; and he went on to argue that each age, in the same way, must have its several Christianity: would not a new form of the faith, he implied, emerge from the scepticism of his own time? Indeed, a proper idealism could be a persuasive ally of religion; for did not all true faith teach us to contemn the unsubstantial shows of the world? 'The first and last lesson of religion,' he was to point out in *Nature*, 'is, "The things that are seen, are temporal; the things that are unseen, are eternal," ' and so, 'It does that for the unschooled, which philosophy does for Berkeley and Viasa.' The reference to Viasa couples Berkeley, as Stewart did in his *Philosophical Essays,* with the far from sceptical idealism of the Hindus, which taught 'the perpetual dependence of the universe . . . on the hand of the Creator.' In a similar vein, the young preacher's first sermon defended the reality of things unseen by suggesting the unreality of things seen. 'Every thoughtful man has felt that there was a more awful reality to thought and feeling, than to the infinite panorama of nature around him. The world . . . seems to him at times, when the intellect is invigorated, to ebb from him, like a sea, and to leave nothing permanent but thought.'[4]

[4] See Appendix, Note C.

In these different ways, the moral sense and the Berkeleian philosophy could do something, even in the 1820's—like his simultaneous doctrine of moral compensation[5]—to help relieve the weight of the unintelligible and unmanageable world and assure him that 'you are the universe to yourself.' Neither of these straws of doctrine, however, was enough to save him from doubt and self-distrust. The moral sense imposed on him a burden of obligation beyond his powers; idealism could relieve him of this, but only by outraging his sense of reality. What assurance they brought him, moreover, could not suffice as long as his faith was attached to an incredible historical revelation, and as long as he felt he must defend it by some process of rational demonstration. The growth of the insight that decisively released him began when he heard the first rumors of a fresh way of viewing the whole problem, the movement of thought he called 'modern philosophy.'

This term is a vague one as Emerson uses it, and must be so to us as well. Take a quantity of Kant; add unequal parts of Goethe, Schiller, Herder, Jacobi, Schleiermacher, Fichte, Schelling, Oken, and a pinch of Hegel; stir in, as Emerson did, a generous amount of Swedenborg; strain through Mme de Staël, Sampson Reed, Oegger, Coleridge, Carlyle, Wordsworth, Cousin, Jouffroy, Constant; spill half and season with Plato— and you have something resembling the indescribable brew called modern philosophy whose aroma Emerson began to detect in his corner of the world in the 1820's, and for which his Puritan-Unitarian-Realist palate slowly but decisively acquired a taste. Much excellent work has been done to trace this influence; our concern here is simply with its effect on his thought.

A long letter to his aunt in 1826 is the first place in his writings, I believe, where we clearly discern the shape of things to come forming beneath his orthodoxy:

Is it not true that modern philosophy by a stout reaction has got to be very conversant with feelings? Bare reason, cold as cucumber, was all that was tolerated in aforetime, till men grew disgusted at the

[5] See pp 34-39.

skeleton & have now given him in ward into the hands of his sister, blushing shining changing Sentiment. . . . Be that as it may, it is one of the *feelings* of modern philosophy, that it is wrong to regard ourselves so much in a *historical* light as we do, putting Time between God & us; and that it were fitter to account every moment of the existence of the Universe as a new Creation, and *all* as a revelation proceeding each moment from the Divinity to the mind of the observer.

He goes on to argue that the strongest evidence for the 'relative truth' of Christianity is its fitness to expound God's moral law to the present generation, whatever its historical authority.

Too much should not be made of this letter. Emerson is still sure that such an appeal to sentiment as a ground for faith is sophistry, and he is still concerned to defend revealed Christianity as an institution. Though the sentiment that it is wrong to put Time between God and us glances ahead strikingly, as Professor Rusk notes, to the Divinity School *Address,* no defense is attempted here of private inspiration. To get around the uncertainty of external evidence, Emerson necessarily appeals to internal evidence—'the moral world as it exists to the man within the breast.' To do so is, of course—though as yet he does not quite see it—to destroy the independent authority of revelation and make it unnecessary. If *all* is a revelation then no particular one is necessary or possible. This notion of a perpetual revelation still seems to him 'Mysticism,' but he is already well along a road that will make it inevitable.

He was brought to it not so much by the problem of the authority of Christianity, however, as through his personal necessities. The winter of 1826-27, for example, which he spent alone in the South, often despondent and sick, facing for all he knew the family fate of an early death, drove home to him his need to know that in his soul he 'walks with God . . . unhurt and immortal.' Newly approbated to preach, 'a moral agent . . . designed to stand in sublime relations to God and to my fellow men,' he must lead a life useless to others. 'What then, young pilot, . . . —art not thyself a castaway?' In these dark days, he put his Christian faith, perforce, to earnest use. That he quite found the support he sought in the 'official consolations' of gospel Christianity is more doubtful. At all events, he learned at this time, as never before, his dependence on a strength beyond his own.

Improving health brought better spirits and showed him not ready for mysticism yet. '. . . we are not to be bound,' he repeated polemically the next fall, 'by suggestions of sentiment, which our reason not only does not sanction, but also condemns.' Little to make us question his loyalty to such reasoning appears on the record in the next two years. In 1830, however, his thought begins to move, until, at the close of that year and the opening of the next, irresistible suggestions of sentiment come on him in a rush. The coincidence of this change with his renewed reading of Coleridge is so striking as to put beyond question who the catalyst was for this transformation, just as the contrast between his expanding self-reliance and Coleridge's unctuous churchliness warns us that Emerson was no man's disciple. Under the stimulus of this new mind, Emerson examines with fresh attention what had long been to him a stirring thought, the doctrine that 'a portion of the Deity lives in men.'

Some of his earlier comments on the near neighborhood of man and God show him carried in his language to suspicious limits. In his first sermon, in which, with the recklessness of the inexperienced preacher, he had poured all his favorite thoughts, he had bidden his congregation remember that God 'is not so much the observer of your actions, as he is the potent principle by which they are bound together: . . . that your reason is God, your virtue is God, and nothing but your liberty, can you call securely and absolutely your own.' A year later, even as he repudiated the notion of a special connection of God with his soul, he went on to exclaim, 'Connexion between God and the Soul,—What is religion but this connexion? . . . Is not this unutterably beautiful and grand, this life within life, this literal Emanuel, *God within us?*' He had been recurrently conscious in his own religious life of 'moments . . . of intercourse with God,' 'insignificant passages' 'which might savour of enthusiasm to an unprepared ear.' Especially the stir-

rings of the moral sense, the voice of God in the heart, had
brought him at times a kindling excitement, as he considered
their implications. 'It seems to me, in obeying them, in squaring
my conduct by them, I part with the weakness of humanity. I
exchange the rags of my nature for a portion of the majesty
of my Maker. . . . I lean on omnipotence.'

Now these scattered suggestions of a connexion between God
and the soul deeper than anything dreamed of in rational
religion began to coalesce in his mind, under the influence of
Coleridge's new point of view, until he cast off his apprehen-
sions and launched from Unitarianism into strange seas of
thought from which he never put back. The change, he felt,
was like day after twilight. The orb of the earth is lighted
brighter and brighter as it turns, until at last there is a particular
moment when the eye sees the sun, and so when the soul perceives God.' Emerson's dawn came when his soul perceived
God in the one place doubt could never reach—in itself.

The 'amazing revelation of my immediate relation to God'
brought him release from 'all the doubts that oppressed me,'
and underlay his break with the Unitarian ministry. We hear
the new note of authority in his voice, for example, in the sermon he preached to his former congregation just after his return
from Europe in 1833. The year before he had justified his
resignation with arguments borrowed from the Quakers against
the Lord's Supper. Now he told them the real reason.

'There is a revolution of religious opinion taking effect around
us as it seems to me the greatest of all revolutions which have
ever occurred that, namely, which has separated the individual
from the whole world and made him demand a faith satisfactory
to his own proper nature, whose full extent he now for the
first time contemplates. . . . Man begins to hear a voice . . .
that fills the heavens and the earth, saying, that God is within
him, that *there* is the celestial host.'

Formulated here in Biblical terms, this great discovery provides us with the simple key to his mature faith and strength.

The rock on which he thereafter based his life was the knowledge that the soul of man does not merely, as had long been taught, contain a spark or drop or breath or voice of God; it *is* God. Such a thought was indeed, as he felt, revolutionary, both in his thought and in his spirit. This book is written to trace its consequences. Before its revelation of the extent of his own proper nature, of the unfailing reservoir of needed strength that lay unsuspected in his own soul, his previous seemingly crushing disabilities evaporated into insignificance. The astonishing surge of pride and confidence that followed, however repugnant to Christians, is a genuine rebirth, and like all such unlooked-for spiritual unfoldings commands our respect and attention. In our literature only Whitman's better-publicized conversion rivals it in interest.

His early subjection to a strong necessity was now, it seemed, entirely transcended. 'In the eye of the philosopher,' he explained in 1837, 'the Individual has ceased to be regarded as a Part, and has come to be regarded as a Whole. He is the World.' On the one hand, to be a Whole confirmed his independence, releasing him in his own mind from dependence for thought and action on his outward relations, and raising to supremacy the virtue of independent judgment. On the other, it brought him an inalienable faith in God, on the authority of his own soul. His problem of authority was solved when he learned from Coleridge to call the reason of the Unitarians the understanding, and to reserve the term reason for the religious sentiments. He thus could repudiate reason in the name of reason: '. . . our Reason is not to be distinguished from the divine Essence.' The problem of evidence could then be solved in five words: 'The faith is the evidence.'

There is obviously a lurking arrogance in this belief in the divinity of the soul to which Emerson was at first particularly sensitive. 'God forbid that I should one moment lose sight of his real eternal Being, of my own dependence, my nothingness whilst yet I dare hail the present deity at my heart.' His new faith prompted humility as well as pride—pride as he thought of the present deity at his heart, humility as he remembered, 'Our

compound nature differences us from God. . . .' No sooner, for
example, does the discovery of a God at the heart of the self
heal the division of God and man, than the self splits in two,
and the old submission to an objective God is repeated within
the sphere of the subjective. The result is his habitual recognition of the 'double consciousness' of man. 'I recognize,' he told
his hearers in 1833, after announcing his revelation, 'I recognize
the distinction of the outer and the inner self—of the double
consciousness . . . ; that is, there are two selfs . . . ; within
this erring passionate mortal self, sits a supreme calm immortal
mind. . . .'

As his new faith takes shape, especially as we see it in his
sermons, it resembles unmistakably the Calvinistic pietism that
Unitarian moralism had left behind—new in that it is based
on a vision of man's power rather than on a conviction of his
sinfulness, but reviving the same sense of the living presence
of a power not our own before which man is nothing. God is
no longer merely 'The most elevated conception of character
that can be formed in the mind'; He is a wind, a light, a stream
—a living power. 'There is one light through a thousand stars.
There is one spirit through myriad mouths,' he wrote in March
1831. '. . . Every word of truth that is spoken by man's lips
is from God. Every thought that is true is from God. Every right
act is from God. . . . There is but one source of power, that is
God.' With the discovery of this source of power within him,
Emerson recovers something of the flame of holy love that the
Puritans had brought to New England two hundred years before.

This fact may help to explain the kinship which every student
of Emerson comes to perceive between him and the greatest
American Calvinist, Jonathan Edwards. A biographer of Edwards has gone so far as to call the philosophy of Emerson
'wholly Edwardian.' Yet the relationship may not seem obvious.
Edwards' great treatises on *The Freedom of the Will* and *The
Nature of True Virtue* were written to demonstrate exactly
what Emerson denied, that man by nature is wholly constrained
by moral inability in a state of sin. True virtue is only possible
through a miraculous infusion of God's grace into the soul,

endowing his elect with a supernatural sense for disinterested benevolence and transforming them from a natural to a spiritual state.

This helpless dependence on grace was repudiated by the Boston liberals. They dwelt lovingly, as Emerson did, on 'The Miracle of Our Being,' since, like a blind man restored to sight, they could not enough admire the new-found fact of human worth. Emerson, though a latecomer at the feast, shares in the rejoicing; but it is not long before he injects into it a new quality. What he wants is what Edwards, what New Englanders, had always wanted, an *assured salvation,* not simply moral capacity. Then if man is not by nature damned, he must be by nature saved. This salvation is what was given him by the revelation of the God within. As Parkes points out, 'the transcendentalist voice of God in the intuition of the heart is merely Edwards' "divine and supernatural light, immediately imparted to the soul by the spirit of God," extended from the elect minority to the human race as a whole.' It has dawned on Emerson, to his joy and amazement, that the perfection which Adam was supposed to have destroyed for all but the few to whom God in his mercy elected to restore it, had never been lost at all. The Fall of Man was a myth. In some men, at some times, God is agent, in the rest latent, but for all 'the whole *is* now potentially in the bottom of his heart.'[6]

In the year 1831 Emerson came into his intellectual majority. His resignation of his charge the next year was simply the inevitable external confirmation of the inner changes of the year before. Beside the self-examination he set down in his journal when he reached the physical age of twenty-one, we should place the self-discovery he composed eight years later on the coming of age of his mind. In July 1831, under the heading 'Gnothi Seauton'—Know Thyself—in an entry so important that he abandoned prose as inadequate to what he had to say, he wrote out, with awkward excitement, the credo of the new Emerson.

[6] See Appendix, Note D.

Written in the first joy of his discovery of the God within,
these lines in their very ungainliness show its immediate consequences with particular plainness: an awe at the presence of the
Infinite within him; a royal pride in this guest that overbore self-
distrust; a sense as well of present unworthiness, and a fresh
incentive to a fitting virtue and greatness; and a solution to the
problem of a faith based on historical revelation. As Cameron
notes, he addresses himself in soliloquy, as it were ventriloquiz-
ing in the voice of the oracle:

If thou canst bear
Strong meat of simple truth,
If thou durst my words compare
With what thou thinkest in the soul's free youth,
Then take this fact unto thy soul,—
God dwells in thee.

    .   .   .   .

Clouded and shrouded there doth sit
The Infinite
Embosomed in a man;
And thou art stranger to thy guest,
And know'st not what thou dost invest.
The clouds that veil his life within
Are thy thick woven webs of sin,
Which his glory struggling through
Darkens to thine evil hue.

Then bear thyself, O man!
Up to the scale and compass of thy guest;
Soul of thy soul.
Be great as doth beseem
The ambassador who bears
The royal presence where he goes.

    .   .   .   .

And in thy closet carry state;
Filled with light, walk therein;
And, as a king
Would do no treason to his own empire,
So do not thou to thine.

    .   .   .   .

Therefore, O happy youth,
Happy if thou dost know and love this truth,
Thou art unto thyself a law,
And since the soul of things is in thee,
Thou needest nothing out of thee.
The law, the gospel, and the Providence,
Heaven, Hell, the Judgment, and the stores
Immeasurable of Truth and Good,
All these thou must find
Within thy single mind,
Or never find. . . .

From this time forward the first principle of his thought was the sufficiency of the single mind. The growth this chapter has followed aimed, with the sureness of a heliocentric plant, at self-reliance, until he could set up the infinitude of the private man as counterpoise to the huge world—to the imperatives of society and the power of fate.[7] Outwardly quiet and deprecatory, this gamble of faith did not lack daring or a quality of high adventure. Twenty years later Melville was to create the archetype of such radical self-reliance in the fated voyage of the Pequod and its ungodly Godlike captain against the White Whale. When Emerson at last openly cut the cords that bound him to society, he also launched out from the slavish shore into the open seas of the mind, a single man against the universe. Fortunately, it turned out that he, unlike Ahab, sailed a sea of which every wave was charmed. But this he could not be sure of for a long time.

Once committed to such a voyage, Emerson could not long remain in the service of a land-bound faith. He stuck it out for another year, but finally, in September 1832, he resigned his pulpit. He did not reach this decision, necessary though it was, without much distress and that winter sailed for a year in Europe to recover his health and peace of mind. He came back

[7] I am speaking here, of course, of the aims of his private thoughts. Personally, though not gregarious, he was always a man of a few strong attachments and deep affections, a temperamentally domestic soul, and one generally careful to give the community its due and more.

confirmed in his independence and thereafter for fourteen years abandoned outward travels to sail the private sea.

The chapters that follow will tell the story of what he found —his first exploration of his new world of thought, his gradual discovery of its hazards, and his eventual mapping and settlement of a home there. At first, swept away by his new vision, he became a prophet of revolution, proclaiming the kingdom of Man with all the fervor of a Ranter or Fifth-Monarchy man. The first section of this book, beginning with Chapter Three, will describe these first years of egoistic challenge and will show what happened when his unlimited claim of power, as it inevitably must, came up against his continuing outer and inner limitations. The second section of the book will show how he contrived to preserve his faith in the Soul in the face of a renewed recognition of the dominion of fate. His chief means to do so turned out to be the most constant of all his articles of faith, one that antedated his discovery of the God within, helped him grow toward it, and was confirmed by it—his trust in the rule of a Moral Law. That will be the subject of the next chapter.

CHAPTER TWO

The Springs of Courage

ON HIS return from Europe, Emerson quickly settled into a congenial way of life, the outwardly placid round of the solitary scholar. After a year at Boston and Newton, he went back to the quiet fields of his fathers at Concord; in September 1835, after his second marriage, he moved into the large white house on the edge of the meadows that was ever afterward to be his home. A legacy from the estate of his first wife that brought him in about $1,200 a year relieved the worst of his fears of poverty, and he supplemented his income by more and more extensive lecturing. Indeed, the coincidental rise of the Lyceum movement with his desertion of the ministry almost vindicates his trust in a beneficent Providence. It provided a timely lay pulpit for his teachings; it forced him to reduce his daily meditations to some sort of order, and thus paved the way for the essays; and throughout his life it provided between a half and a third of his income. Thanks to this largely unforeseen market for his thoughts, he could say, as he wrote to Carlyle in 1838, '. . . here at home, I am a rich man.'

To a substantial degree, his pleasing contrite woodlife permitted him to live by the guiding principle he had set down for himself, again in emphatic verse, as he cut loose from his profession.

> I will not live out of me.
> I will not see with others' eyes;
>
> .   .   .   .
> That which myself delights in shall be Good,
> That which I do not want, indifferent;
> That which I hate is Bad. That's flat.
>
> Henceforth, please God, forever I forego

The yoke of men's opinions. I will be
Light-hearted as a bird and live with God. . . .

No reader of his little poem 'Grace,' dating probably from the same period as the above lines, will suppose that the flat self-trust to which his rejection of a conventional profession stirred him was his only mood at this time or later; we can doubt as little that it was his dominant one. As he once said, when pressed to define his religious position, 'I believe I am more of a Quaker than anything else. I believe in the "still small voice," and that voice is Christ within us,'

To judge by the course of his life, as the years revealed it, his still small voice consistently chose the way of the retired thinker and writer. His inner leading held him faithful, against all doubts, to his literary task. He knew himself best when he wrote to Lydia Jackson—Lidian Emerson to be—in 1835: 'I am born a poet, of a low class without doubt yet a poet. That is my nature & vocation. My singing be sure is very "husky," & is for the most part in prose. Still am I a poet in the sense of a perceiver & dear lover of the harmonies that are in the soul & in matter, & specially of the correspondences between these & those.' Perhaps a better term is the one he found for himself two years later—the scholar. His work in the world was to free imprisoned thoughts and bring them to expression. Charles Emerson was acute and accurate when he claimed that 'he sits among [his thoughts] as the epicure at his long table who would send away no dish untasted. Not that Thoughts are with him things of manufacture of mere merchantable value, no, but works of art, in the finish & perfection of which he is interested as the painter in his landscape or the sculptor in his statue. . . .' The conviction, which *Walden,* for instance, exists to dramatize, that a man can and should *act* on his thoughts, was duly featured among his reflections but had little power to modify his life. His life, fuller and more intense than that given to most of us to achieve, was an inner one, the poet's life of the imagination, an adventure of the mind.

We should not be surprised to find, then, that it was outwardly a quiet life, one that held fast to the conditions that favored its unfolding and resisted any serious urge to reform them. Emerson possessed a strong sense of public responsibility and felt a teacher's and preacher's vocation; his life and thought fell on an 'age of Revolution,' which bedeviled his tender conscience with calls to action; and these things greatly troubled his thoughts. Conscious of the limits of his strength and practical ability, however, he turned out in practice a conservative, in that he remained faithful to his poet's nature and vocation and fell in easily with the circumstances that made its pursuit possible.

Yet his outward quiet belied the ferment and fervor of his thoughts. As we move from his uneventful outward life to the inner life recorded in his journals, we approach the fire under the Andes of his reserve. In the decade or so following his revelation of the God within, when he first explored its startling implications, a deep excitement runs beneath his surface calm and distinguishes this time from his later serenity. If his behavior remained that of a responsible member of established society, his thought had become explosive. To understand what was happening to him, we must examine the intellectual and practical implications of this 'greatest of all revolutions,' as in these years they rapidly expanded in his mind.

❧

Intellectually, Emerson quickly discovered, not without some pleasure, that his new truth flatly contradicted the first principles of common sense. At first, he made some effort to state a consistent doctrine—an effort of which *Nature*, for example, plainly bears the scars. The reason why he soon accepted the fact that he could not succeed appears clearly in a connected series of journal passages, mainly composed in 1835, in which, by means of Coleridge's magic distinction of the Reason and the Understanding, he tried to summarize 'the *first* philosophy, that of mind.'

'Man is conscious,' he begins, 'of a twofold nature which manifests itself in perpetual self-contradiction. Our English philosophers to denote this duality, distinguish the Reason and the Understanding.' This perpetual self-contradiction between the absolute and the actual could easily, with a different emphasis— as Melville's Captain Vere found it, for example—become a tragic one. But Emerson does not find it so, since Reason is his door of access to God. Indeed, Reason is God. 'Our compound nature differences us from God, but our Reason is not to be distinguished from the divine Essence.' This divine principle is what constitutes us men and cannot be alienated from us.

Yet it transcends our individuality: 'A man feels that . . . all the parts of his individual existence, are merely superficial to [this principle].' Man's essence is superhuman. Our existence as we find it in experience is therefore a perpetual anomaly.

> . . . the life of most men is aptly signified by the poet's personi-
> fication, 'Death in Life.' We walk about in a sleep. A few moments
> in the year, or in our lifetime, we truly live; we are at the top of
> our being; we are pervaded, yea, dissolved by the Mind; but we fall
> back again presently. . . . We stand on the edge of all that is great,
> yet are restrained in inactivity and unconscious of our powers. . . .
> We are always on the brink [of an ocean of thought into which we
> do not yet swim].
>
> Much preparation, little fruit. But suddenly in any place, in the
> street, in the chamber, will the heavens open and the regions of
> wisdom be uncovered, as if to show how thin the veil, how null the
> circumstances. As quickly, a Lethean stream washes through us and
> bereaves us of ourselves.

Man is a Janus-faced impossibility, astraddle between two contradictory worlds. Well may Emerson underline his concluding exclamation: '*What a benefit if a rule could be given whereby the mind, dreaming amid the gross fogs of matter, could at any moment* [E]AST ITSELF *and* FIND THE SUN!'

Though this statement is speculative in spirit, in the sense that it represents an effort by Emerson to see his position steadily and to see it whole, it shows little skill or interest in the philosophic endeavor to make *sense* of his dual world. As a matter of fact, at the time he first formulated his position he was on the whole comparatively ignorant of the main documents of Platonic and

Christian speculative mysticism.[1] When all allowance is made for sources, Emerson's position remains substantially a fresh insight of his own, whose nature he worked out initially by inspection without much regard to precedent. Its effect is not unlike that of a primitive in painting.

What makes it fresh is precisely the absence of logical structure. Moving with his times, Emerson has lost the sense of the transcendent. God is related to the world, not as a creator to his creation, but as the soul to the body. Logically, then, he is faced with a choice between two varieties of pantheism: one, pancosmism, the identification of God with the totality of things; the other, acosmism, the denial of the reality of anything except God. Though in his language he often inclined to one or the other of these alternatives, the real peculiarity of his position is that in great part he avoided either one and with considerable honesty remained true to the whole impossible duality of his experience. All the otherworldly connotations of the idea of God live on in full strength in his mind, and all the consequent feeling that to make contact with this supernatural Being is the greatest miracle and the only goal of life; yet the reason for his pardonable excitement is the revelation that this transcendent Power is actually one with his own nature. His is a baffling monistic dualism, or dualistic monism, 'of which any proposition may be affirmed or denied.'

'Who shall define to me an Individual? I behold with awe and delight many illustrations of the One Universal Mind. . . . I can even with a mountainous aspiring say, *I am God.* . . . Yet why not always so? How came the Individual, thus armed and impassioned, to parricide thus murderously inclined, ever to traverse and kill the Divine Life? Ah, wicked Manichee! Into that dim problem I cannot enter. A believer in Unity, a seer of Unity, I yet behold two. . . .

'Cannot I conceive the Universe without a contradiction?' He knew the answer: No. We can see growing in his mind,

[1] See Appendix, Note E.

in the years following his break with his parish, a realization that for him there were two kinds of truth—the intuitions of faith, and the other facts of experience. Though the latter were not properly to be called Truth, which was only revealed to the religious sentiment, they had a stubborn irrefutability of their own, like the rock Dr. Johnson struck with his foot to confute Berkeley; they therefore came to form the basis for a second illegitimate body of truth undreamed of in his first philosophy, whose anomalous existence, when he set his heart on honesty, he was also forced to recognize.

As a result, Emerson's mental self perforce splits into two distinct personalities: the believer, who sees through to the mystical perfection of things, and the detached observer, Mr. Emerson of Concord, who gives their due to facts. Lowell's sharp comment has made this observation a commonplace.

> . . . his is, we may say,
> A Greek head on right Yankee shoulders, whose range
> Has Olympus for one pole, for t'other the Exchange;
> He seems, to my thinking (although I'm afraid
> The comparison must, long ere this, have been made),
> A Plotinus-Montaigne, where the Egyptian's gold mist
> And the Gascon's shrewd wit cheek-by-jowl coexist . . . .

It is less often pointed out that a Plotinus-Montaigne, a seer and Yankee, was something Emerson had to be. Once committed to the enterprise of preserving the faith of a Christian while rejecting the *mythos* that had sustained it, he was forced into the position of becoming his own prophet, as it were, and asserting the truth of what he wanted to believe on his own personal authority. That a part of him held aloof from this enthusiasm is to his credit, as much as that a part was capable of it; his loyalty to fact provided an indispensable ballast to his beliefs and saved him from the mere inanity of the shallower converts to the Newness. The rare tenacity with which he held both to faith and to experience literally split him in two.

'A believer in Unity, a seer of Unity, I yet behold two.' This sentence epitomizes his intellectual position, and helps us understand why he was content to remain in it. The passage from the journals in which it occurs, and the concluding pages of the statement of the first philosophy, are unusual in the 1830's in their concern with the duality of his experience; at this time he was engrossed in seeing Unity, and little impelled to observe the 'two.' The Unity was *there*, that was the grand point. All that really mattered to him, as Goddard has pointed out, was the difference this new truth made in living.

The difference promised to be tremendous—greater than anything that had yet befallen the human race. First of all, it offered him security. God was revealed in his own soul by the best of all possible evidence, the direct experience of his own consciousness. But if God was within him, what could he fear? '. . . because the All is in man, we know that nothing arbitrary, nothing alien shall take place in the universe, nothing contrary to the nature in us. The soul is a party to everything that is, and therefore to everything that shall be done. We pronounce therefore with the voice of fate that such and such things must be, that such and such other things are impossible. . . . Whilst God is external to the soul, it can never be safe or serene, because uncertain what may befal, but having learned to see God far within itself, it shall now be informed of all and is pervaded with a great peace.' What Emerson felt most assured of was the moral government of his world. One might expect such a conviction from a Puritan; a preoccupation with moral law was a badge of the tribe. From earliest youth he had been trained to believe that religion meant above all the acknowledgment of a moral governor and of the sacredness of moral obligation. The Unitarian faith to which he dedicated himself made of morals nearly the whole of religion, as his sermons amply demonstrate. Nor did the new emotional fervor of the faith for which he left his pulpit mean any loss of concern with morals; quite the contrary. The journals of the young ex-Unitarian show him in a veritable ecstasy of moral enthusiasm.

'Milton describes himself . . . as enamoured of moral perfection,' he wrote on shipboard on his way home from Europe. 'He did not love it more than I. That which I cannot yet declare has been my angel from childhood until now. It has separated me from men. It has watered my pillow, it has driven sleep from my bed. It has tortured me for my guilt. It has inspired me with hope. It cannot be defeated by my defeats. It cannot be questioned, though all the martyrs apostatize. It is always the glory that shall be revealed; it is the "open secret" of the universe; and it is only the feebleness and dust of the observer that makes it future, the whole *is* now potentially in the bottom of his heart. It is the soul of religion.' God within, as he once put it, worships God in the universe. Traditional Christianity had, in fact, endangered this worship by tying it to doubtful miracles and revelations lost in the mists of time and had taught it in parables. Now he was face to face with the living law. Officially at least, Emerson abandoned the service of the Christian God for no other purpose than to testify better by his words and by his life to the self-subsistent reality of the Moral Law.

Here again, his new faith only completed a train of thought begun much earlier. Before he had dared to dream of a God within, he had found a basis for asserting the rule of law, in his beloved principle of Compensation.

'Ever since I was a boy,' he began his 1841 essay on this theme, 'I have wished to write a discourse on Compensation . . .'; and in fact the earliest entry in his published journals that clearly asserts this principle is one with which he reeopened his journals, after a lapse following his graduation, in the winter of his first schoolteaching year, at the age of eighteen. The principle of compensation represents Emerson's first and most explicit attempt to cite objective evidence of a truth he could not live without, that 'all things are moral.'

On the one hand it was a doctrine of retribution. Christianity, of course, had its own doctrine of inevitable retribution in another world. But Emerson's need was to establish a belief that justice is done here. Hence, 'Instead of denouncing a future contingent vengeance, I see that vengeance to be contemporary with the crime.' He elaborates this claim in the essay. 'Every act rewards itself . . . in a twofold manner; first in the thing, or in real nature; and secondly in the circumstance, or in apparent nature. . . . The causal retribution is in the thing and is seen by the soul.' The state of mind that permits the commission of a crime is itself the punishment: 'Inasmuch as [the criminal] carries the malignity and the lie with him he so far deceases from nature.' In the mood of high ethical idealism which his essay strikes he can hold that 'this deadly deduction makes square the eternal account.'

At the same time, he by no means dropped his belief that 'In some manner there will be a demonstration of the wrong to the understanding also. . . .' The theory of internal retribution, we can see, had one serious flaw, namely, that those most deserving of it were least likely to be sensible of it. So a stern retributive refrain also runs through his enunciation of his law. Evildoers are inevitably detected and punished, not just in the next world, but in this. Wrong never wins even the material advantages for which it aims. He deploys his twofold punishment, in the thing and in the circumstance, in such a way that both will unite to enforce the lesson of the futility of wrong and the inevitability of retribution. The aim and upshot of all is to teach, with all the strength he can muster of rhetoric and example, 'that ancient doctrine of Nemesis, who keeps watch in the universe and lets no offence go unchastised.'

On the other hand, compensation guaranteed to him the inevitable reward of good. Here his stress is on the reward in real nature rather than in the circumstance. Not that he is indifferent to or means to deny the proposition that the good man is happy; far from it. '. . . you cannot do [the good man] any harm; . . . disasters of all kinds, as sickness, offence, poverty, prove benefactors. . . .' But Emerson rejects the thought of reward in the circumstance much more easily than that of punishment. At the start of his essay, for example, he ridicules the base tone of popular theology, which seemed to teach that the good will be compensated in the next life with the same 'bank-stock and doubloons, venison and champagne' which sinners enjoy now.

'What is the reward of virtue? Virtue.' This marginal note in his New Testament, probably dating from his Divinity School days, is the sum and substance of his thought on the matter. Thus he must argue, at the conclusion of his essay, 'There is no penalty to virtue; no penalty to wisdom; they are proper additions of being.' Material success, if he could get it, might reconcile the bad man to his loss of being; additions of being do permit the good man to rise above his fortunes. While insisting, then, 'All things shall be added unto [the virtuous soul],' Emerson shows in places more than a little Stoic or Puritan toughness. The good man cannot, he claims, suffer any harm; but apparently he can be burned at the stake, where he is to console himself with the reflection that he cannot be dishonored. This may be to affirm an Optimism, but it is not soft.

The notion of an automatic moral compensation, nevertheless, is without question the most unacceptable of Emerson's truths, and a major cause of his present decline of reputation. He confronts simultaneously two classic human problems—the relation of virtue to happiness, and the problem of evil—and seemingly proceeds to deny that they *are* problems. With Melville, we like men who dive, but not when they come up to report that deep water is an illusion. Certainly there are compensations to many evils; there is a price, often too high a one, on most goods; integrity does sometimes have its rewards; some crime does not pay. We can fairly agree that there must have been, so far, *some* balance of good and ill, or we would be already extinct. But Emerson pushed his principle far beyond these modest consolations.

One reason he did so was to supply his need for a secular gospel. His aim in these early reflections was the same as that of Christian apologists for more than a century before him: to establish the essential articles of religion on a basis independent of tradition or revelation. Like them, he enlisted the aid of that authority whose rise was largely responsible for the weakening of religion—natural science. 'The heart of the Enlightenment,' Herbert Schneider has said, '. . . was the marriage of natural science with morals and religion.' By this definition Emerson's conception of 'moral science' is an Enlightenment idea. Parallel with natural science, he held, it was possible to construct a moral science, equally exact, equally unquestionable. 'The Teacher that I look for and await shall enunciate with more precision and universality . . . those beautiful yet severe compensations that give to moral nature an aspect of mathematical science.' For the time being, as historical Christianity lost its authority with him, this aspect of mathematical science was the chief sanction of his faith in a moral law.

For a few years, moreover, compensation played an indispensable part in furthering his emancipation from scepticism and self-distrust; the assertion of a law of compensation is the first major offensive action in his private battle with fate.

From it, for example, he derived the lesson, 'The man is all.' We take the place and rank to which our character entitles us; character determines fortune. More, character *is* fortune; an inner advance compensates for any outer failure. By this logic, '. . . every misfortune is misconduct, . . . every honour is desert. . . .' In the words he attributed to St. Bernard, 'Nothing can work me damage except myself; the harm that I sustain I carry about with me, and never am a real sufferer but by my own fault.' A retreat to such congenital Stoicism, as to some impregnable inner redoubt, became a habitual tactic with him whenever the problems of freedom in a world of fate pressed him too closely; appropriately, it is the first position he took up in his initial advance toward independence.

If the moralistic reflex was easy, however, it was also narrow and dogmatic; and it brought with it a sometimes onerous pressure of obligation. The young Emerson, especially, was highly, sometimes almost morbidly, self-critical, sharply conscious of numerous shortcomings which easily took on a coloring of guilt and sin. Clearly the genial thought of an inevitable reward for the adoption in act of a great sentiment had no power to help him through the times when he felt his incapacity to do any such thing. At such moments he took comfort in a wider reading of compensation.

His little poem 'Compensation,' for example, gracefully justifies his stiffness and idleness:

> Why should I keep holiday
> When other men have none?
> Why but because, when these are gay,
> I sit and mourn alone?
>
> And why, when mirth unseals all tongues,
> Should mine alone be dumb?
> Ah! late I spoke to silent throngs,
> And now their hour is come.

So he met the uncontrollable ups and downs of his spirits with an appeal to compensation. 'The principle of repairs is in us, the remedial principle. Everybody perceives greatest contrasts in his own spirit and powers. To-day he is not worth a brown cent, to-morrow he is better than a million. . . . When, therefore, I doubt and sin, I will look up at the moon, and remembering that its errors are all periodical; I will anticipate the return of my own spirits and faith.'

As he invoked this principle to meet his inner inadequacies, so he used it as an amulet against outer misfortune. It did not by any means assure him success, but it did teach 'the indifferency of circumstances.' Essentially it was a principle of perspective. Against any particular failure or loss or fear—against any success or gain—he was to set the larger view and learn to be content; in the long run, things ironed themselves out. Fate was no arbitrary tryant but obeyed a law. Hence his early welcome for this seemingly rather bleak principle; it allayed the instinctive anxiety for the future—charmed the child in the soul, as Plato put it—and so helped him win the confidence he needed to live his own life. 'Herein I rejoice with a serene eternal peace,' he wrote in the essay. 'I contract the boundaries of possible mischief.'

Clearly, however, as a faith to live by, compensation had its limitations. It was inherently a defensive faith, a counterpunch; it could teach the indifferency of circumstances, for example, but not their beneficence. The reward it guaranteed for virtue, to be sure, was an exception, but here the limitation was the moral condition put on good fortune. We can understand, then, that when Emerson found a basis for the assertion of unconditional good, in his discovery of the God within the soul, the law of compensation slipped to a subordinate place in his thoughts. Then his inner limitations virtually evaporated before his limitless possibilities; and the outer world glowed with a vast promise in which all things were tuned and set to good. A creed that could be reduced, as he once wrote, to the single article, 'Goodness is the only Reality,' clearly underwrote his security much more handsomely than the minimum coverage provided by compensation.

The ethical gospel he derived from this revelation became the core of his religious teachings: that the moral nature of man is his constitutive part; that in Reality he is 'nothing else than a capacity for justice, truth, love, freedom, power'; and that at the same time moral perfection rules the world, every part and particle of which, in Reality, obeys a moral law. The only meaningful religious question was the relation of a man to this Reality, of the individual visible existence in the meaningless world of fact to the moral law without and moral nature within.

This triumphant faith, however, only intensified a confusion already apparent in his thought on compensation. The distinction between the moralistic and the consolatory applications of that principle reappears magnified in his larger conception of 'moral nature.'

In *Nature*, in a well-known passage, he proclaimed, 'All things are moral; and . . . hint or thunder to man the laws of right and wrong, and echo the Ten Commandments.' Nature replaced Scripture as a revelation of our duty and an encouragement to moral effort. But when, as in an equally familiar passage in the Divinity School *Address*, he taught the 'assurance that Law is sovereign over all natures,' he had a different point in mind. The purpose of the *Address* is to announce 'the sublime creed that the world is not the product of manifold power, but of one will, of one mind; . . . and whatever opposes that will is everywhere balked and baffled, because things are made so, and not otherwise.' Man's peace and fulfillment, it followed, lay in an utter submission. 'When we enter upon the domain of LAW, we do indeed come out into light. To him who, by God's grace, has seen that by being a mere tunnel or pipe through which the divine Will flows, he becomes great, and becomes a Man,—the future wears an eternal smile, and the flight of time is no longer dreadful. I assure myself always of needed help, and go to the grave undaunted because I go not to the grave. I am willing also to be as passive to the great forces I acknowledge as is the thermometer or the clock, and quite part with all will as superfluous.'

Now, something that thunders to us the Ten Commandments does not encourage us to part with all will as superfluous. We have here another characteristic Emersonian fusion, or superposition, of traditional distinctions. He has identified what his ancestors carefully kept apart—God's revealed will and his secret will, the moral and the natural law. As Perry Miller has explained, 'The soul of Puritan theology is the hidden God, who is not fully revealed even in His own revelation. The Bible is His declared will; behind it always lies His secret will. . . . His secret will is His decree of what shall be, His revealed will is His command of what ought to be. . . . Undoubtedly the two are not in fact opposed, but . . . according to our experience, they . . . can often seem thoroughly contradictory.' By means of this distinction Puritans thought they prevented the imperatives of the moral law from being weakened by contradictory experience.

Emerson's law had no such protection. His moral law was the law of nature; what ought to be is what shall be; 'the best is the true.' It was really only by an incomplete understanding of his own thought that the nature of things could seem to echo the Ten Commandments. The truer inference from the fact of law was that 'we are begirt with laws which execute themselves.'

His position is summed up in a sentence from 'Spiritual Laws': 'Virtue is the adherence in action to the nature of things and the nature of things makes it prevalent [i.e., makes it prevail].' His faith in the dominion of the moral law, then, tended at need to slide off into a faith in automatic Beneficence, with continuing consequences in the development of his thought.[2]

A parallel confusion appears in his conception of virtue, man's obedience to law. For the Unitarian, virtue was simply right action, a conscious obedience to conscience. The moral life was a process of self-improvement, a slow growth, by effort and self-discipline, not unassisted by grace, in the ability to obey the laws of right and wrong. But with the emergence of Emerson's new piety, which was, in the manner described in the last chapter, both a revival and a reversal of the piety of the Puritans, virtue became no longer simply a matter of behavior; it was a new state of being, a natural state of grace. A divine power for sanctity was in the heart of every man by nature.

In reaching his comforting conviction, therefore, that the moral nature of man is perfect virtue, and that the whole *is* now, Emerson rather thoroughly undermined the moralism with which he started. As he came to feel, 'there is a kind of descent and accommodation felt when we leave speaking of moral nature to urge a virtue which it enjoins. To the well-born child all the virtues are natural, and not painfully acquired. Speak to his heart, and the man becomes suddenly virtuous.' Virtue was simply a surrender to nature, a 'simple rise as by specific levity . . . into the region of all the virtues.' Emerson's moral efforts, after his Unitarian days, were concentrated both on right action, and on the means and possibility of this simple rise.

The worship of moral perfection, then, for which he deserted the Unitarian God, had two aspects, generally not distinguished in his own mind, one deriving from the moralistic discipline of Unitarianism, the other from the tradition of Calvinistic piety— one the sense of duty, conscience, moral injunction, the law; the other the power to *obey* the law, the sentiment of virtue. God enters the soul to teach it duty; and God also enters the soul to

[2] See Part II, esp pp. 123-40 and pp. 143-45.

enable it to do its duty. The two aspects are distinguished, for example, in his Civil War quatrain:

> So nigh is grandeur to our dust,
> So near is God to man,
> When Duty whispers low, *Thou must,*
> The youth replies, *I can.*

Virtue was a mode of behavior to which men were admonished by conscience; and virtue was a state of being from which virtuous actions would flow by nature. It was *Thou must* and *I can;* law and power; discipline and nature.

The faith at which Emerson thus arrived, as paradoxical as it was exalted, is best exhibited in that address in which he tried most directly to formulate his new religion, the Divinity School *Address.* Firmly substituting nature for revelation as the ground of faith, it is a solemn celebration of that moral law and moral sentiment which constitute the Reality of nature. = *Creation*

It opens with a hymn to the perfection and bounty of visible nature. By its incantation the indifferent nature of our ordinary experience is transmuted into a holy scene in which every sight and sound conspires to bless and ease the human spirit. '. . . The air is full of birds, and sweet with the breath of the pine, the balm-of-Gilead, and the new hay. Night brings no gloom to the heart with its welcome shade. Through the transparent darkness the stars pour their almost spiritual rays. . . .' It is with no jar or effort that we move from this visible perfection to an insight of the perfection of the laws of the soul, agreeing without protest in such an atmosphere 'that to the good, to the perfect, [man] is born, low as he now lies in evil and weakness'; and from this it is a small step to an intuition of the indwelling Supreme Spirit, who sees to it that Law is sovereign over all natures.

The perception of this law of laws, awakening the religious sentiment, then becomes naturally the sole content of religion and the foundation of morals, his response to it lifting man spontaneously into virtue. 'When in innocency or when by intellectual perception he attains to say,—"I love the Right; Truth is beautiful within and without for evermore. Virtue, I am thine; save me; use me; thee will I serve, day and night, in great, in small, that I may be not virtuous, but virtue;"—then is the end of the creation answered, and God is well pleased.' Against the background of a nature thus impregnated with moral perfection the myths and rituals of historical Christianity look like childish allegory—and Emerson is careful to keep the contrast vivid. '. . . the word Miracle, as pronounced by Christian churches, gives a false impression; it is Monster. It is not one with the blowing clover and the falling rain.' 'Let [the dialogues of Christ] lie as they befell, alive and warm, part of human life and of the landscape and of the cheerful day.' 'The faith should blend with the light of rising and of setting suns, with the flying cloud, the singing bird, and the breath of flowers. But now the priest's Sabbath has lost the splendor of nature. . . .'

Indications meanwhile are not lacking that the sweet, natural goodness with which he would replace the vaunting, overpowering, excluding sanctity of sectarian religion has its own austerity, as when he asserts that 'the soul of the community . . . wants nothing so much as a stern, high, stoical, Christian discipline, to make it know itself and the divinity that speaks through it.' Yet such is his artistry, such his power of conviction, that while still within the circle of this charm we are hard put to it not to accept as altogether reasonable the fantastic paradox he would teach, that purity and strict conscience are *more natural* than the dreary years of routine and of sin that are the common lot. So at the end we respond with something of his devotion as he calls for a 'new Teacher that . . . shall see the identity of the law of gravitation with purity of heart; and shall show that the Ought, that Duty, is one thing with Science, with Beauty, and with Joy.' The whole address, in the rapt dexterity with which it claims all the spontaneity of nature without giving up any of the discipline of morals, is a considerable *tour de force,* and a most revealing example of Emerson's highly Puritanical rebellion against Puritanism.

The pattern revealed here controls Emerson's thought on law throughout his life: a high Stoical moralistic emphasis on the surface; beneath it, a more personal insistence on a reign of Good in nature that contracts the boundaries of possible mischief and assures him his peace. I shall not have much more to say about Emerson as a moralist. His ethical teachings, though unquestionably edifying, and valuable in their aphoristic force, are on the whole neither original nor specific enough to command particular attention. What is interesting in his thought can usually be discussed without much reference to virtue and moral law; that fact is one reason why his thought is interesting.

Emerson himself, however, would spurn such a statement. Though he may at times, for convenience, appear to think in his shirt sleeves, like Whitman, and take the open road of nature, his moral frock coat is always within reach, ready to slip on at any moment, as easy and familiar as a second nature. Everything in the rest of this book, it should be understood, is to be read under the invisible running title: 'All things are moral.' The sense of higher laws running through nature, and an aspiration to the natural purity they demand, operates as a perpetual balance wheel to all his speculations and habitually colors his thought on any topic.

There is a concealed upper level to life, he felt, a region of all the virtues, forever opposing its original freshness and innocency to the gross worldliness of ordinary living. It was as if our common life were confined to the thick and fat atmosphere of a closed and crowded room. Open a window, Emerson came to tell us; step outside into your native immortal air. Man lives slackly in the valleys when he is born for the heights. He found the perfect image for his Stoical ideal in the mountain Monadnock.

> [I] think how Nature in these towers
> Uplifted shall condense her powers,
>
> .   .   .   .   .   .
>
> The Indian cheer, the frosty skies,
> Rear purer wits, inventive eyes,—
>
> .   .   .   .   .   .
>
> Man in these crags a fastness find
> To fight pollution of the mind;

In the wide thaw and ooze of wrong,
Adhere like this foundation strong,
The insanity of towns to stem
With simpleness for stratagem.

Heights like these, however, were not to be scaled every day. In his daily living the thought of the rule of law acted, in the excellent phrase Haniel Long uses of Whitman, as one of his chief 'springs of courage.' Grounded in this, he could relegate all Terror to the 'exterior life,' as he does in his revealing lecture on 'The Tragic.' The same repudiation of tragedy emerges as the theme of the remorseless closing pages of 'Compensation,' which are content to find the compensations of calamity in the growth of character. Prosperity, not calamity, is the enemy of the soul, whose law is inner growth. The 'happier mind' will be forever 'quitting its whole system of things, its friends and home and laws and faith,' for 'the riches of the soul,' until 'all worldly relations hang very loosely about him.' This progress is aided by disaster. 'A fever, a mutilation, a cruel disappointment. . . . The death of a dear friend, wife, brother, lover,'—and Emerson is surely remembering his own lost wife and brothers—such a loss is really a benefit, in that 'it commonly operates revolutions in our way of life, terminates an epoch of infancy or of youth which was waiting to be closed, breaks up a wonted occupation, or a household, or style of living, and allows the formation of new ones more friendly to the growth of character.' Again the reference to Ellen, and the revolution in his way of life and wonted occupation which her death helped to further, is impossible to miss. Emerson is speaking from the heart, teaching his own hard-tested secret of insulation from calamity: Live in the Soul. The sharper the hurt, the better it serves to break our worldly ties, shatter the barriers we throw up between too much and me, and whip us willy-nilly into self-sufficiency, alone with the Alone.

The hardness of the saints! From this powerful and chilling idealism, before which a dearly loved and fondly remembered young wife becomes but one 'dead circumstance' the more, it is only a step to the round denials of the reality of evil which we find in the Divinity School *Address* and elsewhere. Clearly this line of thought has a New England physiognomy; it is a chip off the block of Puritan 'optimism.' Its immediate ancestor is the Unitarian solution to the problem of evil, as summarized by Emerson, for example, in 1826: 'The doctrine of immortality, the grand revelation of Christianity, . . . solves the question concerning the existence of evil. For if man is immortal, this world is his place of discipline and the value of pain is then disclosed.' When Emerson's belief in immortality reluctantly yielded to translation into spiritual terms, he clung to his assurance that man was somehow shielded from final and irremediable evil.

The result, of course, was to deny his philosophy the tragic sense of life, to its consequent impoverishment, as well as to betray him into saying some foolish or shallow things. But this limitation was the unavoidable price of his experiment in self-reliance. Tragedy is a recognition of limitations, while the philosophy that sustained Emerson was a denial of them, a romantic emancipation of the private man that depended on his ability to believe that 'the absolutely trustworthy was seated at [his] heart.' Hence, though he could and did recognize the empirical existence of evil, he could never admit its 'Reality' without striking at the root of his confidence. There is plenty of this *inverse* recognition of evil in Emerson. His famous assertion in 'Experience' of the unreality of his devastating grief for his son is the most impressive illustration of the necessity he was under to protect, at whatever human cost, his hard-won security.

We begin to live only when we have conceived life as tragedy, Yeats has said. The opposite was true of Emerson. Only as he refused to conceive life as tragedy could he find the courage to live the self-dependent life he required.

❦

The God within, however, offered Emerson not simply a great peace, but a great hope. The doctrine of the infinitude of the private man was the point of agitation in his thought, the flame under the pot, because it irresistibly suggested that the power newly disclosed within his own soul might, now that it was at last recognized, be made to flood his whole being and sweep away his duality with it. No inference was more deceptively easy to draw. If there is no bar or wall in the soul, where man, the effect, ceases, and God, the cause, begins, what hinders man from being a 'creator in the finite'? His intuitions speak to him of a Love, Freedom, Power which *is* now potentially at the bottom of the heart. Then why not realize it in every sense and be done with his unaccountable individuality once and for all? Under the spur of this electrifying plausibility, the old dream of an imminent millennium, that had turned so many Christian heads, touches Emerson's imagination also, and for a while we watch a man who is a little beside himself with hope.

During these few years he himself experienced the Saturnalia or excess of faith which he later identified as transcendentalism. A word, a deed, a thought more anywhere might turn the trick, and man as he really is burst fullgrown into day. His sense that we stand on the edge of all that is great is so insistent that he feels a kind of bewildered impatience that his translation should still delay. Nothing stands between man and God; yet how persistent that 'nothing' is! What is this Lethe men have drunk, that they cling to their lethargy when an ocean of power lies open before them? 'I call it self-distrust—a fear to launch away into the deep, which they might freely and safely do. It is as if the dolphins should float on rafts, or creep and squirm along the shore in fear to trust themselves to the element which is really native to them.' No sooner has he won free of the old mythological delusion of the Fall, than he finds himself compelled to spin new fables to account for the delay of his visible perfection. 'The generic soul in each individual is a giant overcome with sleep which locks up almost all his senses, and only leaves him a little superficial animation. Once in an age at hearing some deeper voice, he lifts his iron lids . . . : then is he obeyed like a God, but quickly the lids fall, and sleep returns.'

The keynote of this period of aroused expectation is struck

in *The American Scholar.* The revolutionary force of this historic address is somewhat disguised for the modern reader by the decorum of Emerson's tone, which is, as Firkins notes, academic and clerical throughout. Emerson's enthusiasm burns with a dry light that gives no warmth. Characteristically, at this high point of his time of power and hope, the tone of his greatest call to arms suggests reservations not apparent in the matter and reminds us that the whole man is even now not committed to the enterprise. Even so, his secret thought is unmistakable.

> . . . The world is nothing, the man is all; . . . in yourself slumbers the whole of Reason; it is for you to know all; it is for you to dare all. Mr. President and Gentlemen, this confidence in the unsearched might of man belongs, by all motives, by all prophecy, by all preparation, to the American Scholar. . . . thousands of young men . . . do not yet see, that if the single man plant himself indomitably on his instincts, and there abide, the huge world will come round to him. Patience,—patience; with the shades of all the good and great for company; and for solace the perspective of your own infinite life; and for work the study and the communication of principles, the making those instincts prevalent, the conversion of the world. . . . A nation of men will for the first time exist, because each believes himself inspired by the Divine Soul which also inspires all men.

Even now one instinctively responds for the moment to the promise in these words, which prick and sting all we have of manhood and ambition. At the same time, the deeper hope from which their urgency springs is almost beyond our ability to recapture, even in imagination. Yet Emerson's dream of redeeming man from human limitations, plainly advanced in *The American Scholar,* was then utterly serious. Though not quite ready himself to give up to the soul beyond the possibility of a quick self-recovery, the thought then central to his mind was of a new state of life, a state of greatness and freedom beyond anything in human experience, into which, if he could only hit upon the password, he and all men might at any moment enter.

Emerson's inclination to think of this new state as one of new purity and virtue was generally greatest when he was most conservative in mood. Involving, as it necessarily did, a submission to the code of the community, this was the emphasis in his new teaching that was most acceptable to his society, the one that grew most directly from the faith he had abandoned. So we find his greatest emphasis on moral nature and moral sentiment, as we might expect, in the first formative years of the 1830's, when he was closest in spirit to traditional Christianity; and again in the 1850's and after, when his chief topic of discussion had become the conduct of life. Less constantly stressed at other times, the moral reading of his faith was not at all qualified or given up, but lay ready to hand as the preacher and moralist in Emerson required it.

A deep conflict, however, between his need for power and freedom, and his aspiration to purity, is dissolved in his faith in the Soul, but not resolved there. Rather his thought of the Soul obeys a basic polarity, swinging at need from the ideal of Power at one extreme to Law at the other—*life* and *moral perfection*. The two meanings are no less distinct because he usually identified them. As a man he valued freedom; as a Puritan he valued purity; his faith in the Soul promised him both but did not make them the same thing. To see the whole quality of his rebellion against tradition, therefore, we need to look beneath the moralistic language in which he was always ready to formulate it and discern the radical egoistic anarchism it sanctioned and masked.

CHAPTER THREE

The Dream of Greatness

THE best-known statement of the radical self-dependence Emerson required is, of course, his essay 'Self-Reliance,' in which he wove together an anthology of passages on this theme from his lectures and journals of the previous eight years. A childlike security in the dominion of Good is here scornfully rejected.

> Cast the bantling on the rocks,
> Suckle him with the she-wolf's teat,
> Wintered with the hawk and fox,
> Power and speed be hands and feet.

Security begins when a man cuts loose from dependence on any foreign force and lives wholly from within. 'The man must be so much that he must make all circumstances indifferent.' Emerson's imagination is stirred with the thought of a radical recovery of natural freedom, a vigor of wild virtue released from the inhibitions of a society entrenched in establishments and forms. The essay is a Spartan fife to rouse the hearer from dreams of needed help and throw him back on his wild Gentile stock of courage and constancy. Virtue in this context is not purity but *virtus*, the manliness proper to man in his integrity.

The basis for his belief in the possibility of recovering such manliness is still, of course, the doctrine of the God within. The Trustee is 'the aboriginal Self, on which a universal reliance may be grounded.' The essay calls on man to ground his life on this aboriginal Self and in this way to render himself invulnerable to all the exterior life. 'He who knows that power is inborn, that he is weak because he has looked for good out of him and elsewhere, and, so perceiving, throws himself unhesitatingly on his thought, instantly rights himself, stands in the erect position, commands his limbs, works miracles; just as a man who stands on his feet is stronger than a man who stands on his head.' With this Power to draw on, men are 'not minors and invalids in a protected corner, not cowards fleeing before a revolution, but guides, redeemers and benefactors, obeying the Almighty effort and advancing on Chaos and the Dark.'

Such Self-reliance (the capital letter must always be understood) is clearly not the same in mood as the religious sentiment, the glad submission to the dominion of the law that we examined in the last chapter, even though both are mutually reconcilable inferences from the same doctrine. According to the second, the Soul within is the Universal, the One Mind that unites all men, the Reason or moral nature of mankind, in which all private peculiarities are forgotten; in so far as man obeys it he leaves his individuality behind. According to the first, on the other hand, it is an original intuition of the private man, a principle of independence, creativity and youth, the mainspring of all heroism and greatness; in this sense, 'the Individual is the World.' If the one stresses the divinity of the Soul, as opposed to the weakness of mortal nature, the other stresses the subjectiveness of the Soul, as opposed to all external power or authority.

'The subject is the receiver of Godhead . . . ; nor can any force of intellect attribute to the object the proper deity which sleeps or wakes forever in every subject.' Thanks to his proper deity, the individual is free, entire, sovereign, master of the finite. In the past the Church—society—had been the mediator between God and the erring private man; now, with God within man, the 'me of me,' Church and society became a cumbersome distraction, useful, if at all, only in the way the State, perhaps all nature, was useful, as a means of educating the soul drenched in time to step into his heritage. Properly, the man is all.

This radical egoism is expounded with unusual sharpness in Emerson's characterization of 'The Transcendentalist,' his degree of dramatic disengagement in that lecture permitting him to dispense with protective qualification.

. . . His thought,—that is the Universe. His experience inclines him to behold the procession of facts you call the world, as flowing perpetually outward from an invisible, unsounded centre in himself, centre alike of him and of them, and necessitating him to regard all things as having a subjective or relative existence, relative to that aforesaid Unknown Centre of him.

. . . All that you call the world is the shadow of that substance which you are, the perpetual creation of the powers of thought, of those that are dependent and of those that are independent of your will. . . . You think me the child of my circumstances: I make my circumstance.

Though less often dwelt on, in the whole body of his public writings, than his more moralistic and reverential reflections, this transfer of the world into the consciousness is the secret key that unlocked his energies. The revelation of what it meant to be a Man, of the unlimited resources of spiritual energy inherent in his separate and independent self, is the vision that charges his three challenges of the 1830's—*Nature, The American Scholar,* the Divinity School *Address*—with their immense store of force, and creates the unsettling impression they manage to convey that a revolutionary reversal of values is just about to take place. The magnitude and direction of the challenge may be shown by an analysis of *Nature,* his most sustained and serious attempt to formulate his philosophical and religious position.

Since *Nature* is written under several strong and not always harmonious influences—Coleridge, Swedenborg, and various varieties of Platonism—and since it discusses such an array of elaborately subdivided topics, one cannot always easily penetrate its rapid criss-cross of ideas and see its underlying intention. A comparison with the contemporary journals, however, makes plain that Emerson's inquiry into the meaning and purpose of nature is at bottom an effort to assimilate nature into himself, to reduce the NOT ME to the ME. The effort took two directions: one, toward the conquest of nature intellectually, by achieving her Idea or theory; the other, toward a practical conquest, a kingdom of man, by learning the lesson of power. Through most of the book the first is dominant; the aim of the book is to indicate an answer to the question, To what end is nature? His chief weapon for this conquest of nature is idealism, a word he uses in two senses: the Ideal Theory of the Locke-Berkeley-Hume tradition; and a more Platonic conception.

The first five chapters are designed to establish the dominion of Platonic Ideas over nature. A soon discarded Swedenborgian notion of nature as a kind of divine cryptogram, a mute gospel which man is to decipher, somewhat obscures this purpose in *Nature,* but it emerges clearly in a summary entered in his journals at about the time he was putting the book together for the press. 'The delight that man finds in classification is the first index of his Destiny. He is to put nature under his feet by a knowledge of Laws. . . . The moment an idea is introduced among facts the God takes possession. . . . Thus through nature is there a striving upward. Commodity points to a greater good. Beauty is nought until the spiritual element. Language refers to that which is to be said. Finally; Nature is a discipline, and points to the pupil and exists for the pupil. Her being is subordinate; his is superior; Man underlies Ideas. Nature receives them as her God.'

Up to this point Emerson has not gone much farther than a Cambridge Platonist or a Unitarian might have gone, though he has undoubtedly expressed himself differently. He has asserted the primacy of Ideas, has called this world a place of discipline, and has read man's moral values into his environment. He portrays a man, however, still in a state of pupilage, environed with a parentally superior nature, even if she is centered on him; and he has done little to suggest that the common God of man and nature is not the familiar external Creator, playing his master role in the drama of Christendom. From this subordination he breaks loose in the last three chapters, using the sceptical sense of idealism as a lever. Here he accomplishes his real revolution. Outside is subjected to inside; the huge world comes round to the man.

First, by means of the Ideal Theory, he would lead us 'to regard nature as phenomenon, not a substance; to attribute necessary existence to spirit; to esteem nature as an accident and an effect.' Nature is brought within the sphere of the self; man

is finally cut adrift from the belief in any reality external to
himself. But to affirm the lack of a reality outside was only half
the truth, unless reality were rediscovered inside; so Emerson
moves from idealism to spiritualism. 'The Idealist says, God
paints the world around your soul. The spiritualist saith, Yea,
but lo! God is within you. The self of self creates the world
through you. . . .' Thus the final revelation, reached in the
chapter 'Spirit,' is the oneness of man and the self of self, so
that man, the self, can be considered in a certain sense not merely
the pupil or the observer but the creator of nature. Here, of
course, the distinction springs up between the universal man
and the individual; as things are, the self of self seems infinitely
to transcend the capacities of the individual. But the distinction
is a secondary or relative one, between possibility and actuality,
and not between two separate things; the thought that stirs
Emerson is that God is essentially self, and that ideally or poeti-
cally the two should and can be identical.

This ultimate assimilation of God into the self is the vision
of the orphic poet in 'Prospects.' Whatever the relation of these
passages to the conversation of Alcott, they are clearly integral
to Emerson's book and Emerson's thought. The orphic poet is a
device for expressing certain of Emerson's insights too bold and
visionary to be asserted in his own person. Where expository
prose, tied down to common sense, falters, the freer and more
irresponsible speech of the poet can complete the thought. And
the thought the orphic poet expresses for his creator is the ideal
identity of man and God.

'Nature is not fixed but fluid. Spirit alters, moulds, makes it.
. . . Every spirit builds itself a house, and beyond its house a
world, and beyond its world a heaven. . . . Build therefore your
own world. . . . The kingdom of man over nature, which cometh
not with observation,—a dominion such as now is beyond his
dream of God,—he shall enter without more wonder than the
blind man feels who is gradually restored to perfect sight.' At
the same time the poet spins a myth of the fall of man, to account
for man's present compound nature. Emerson regularly moves
into mythology when speaking of this duality—necessarily, since

his philosophy denies it. Why is man not divine in fact as well as in nature? There is no answer from philosophy, but the poet can interpose a fable. 'A man is a god in ruins. . . . Once he . . . filled nature with his overflowing currents. Out from him sprang the sun and moon. . . . But, having made for himself this huge shell, his waters retired; he no longer fills the veins and veinlets; he is shrunk to a drop. . . . Yet sometimes he starts in his slumber, and wonders at himself and his house, and muses strangely at the resemblance betwixt him and it.'

In this chapter, also, the intellectual and the practical conquests of nature come together. Why can we not discover the secret of nature? 'The reason why . . . is because man is disunited with himself.' We shall find a theory of nature when we achieve the redemption of the soul. And the same self-fulfillment will solve the question of power. The momentary exhibitions of man's proper dominion over things that we now glimpse in acts of heroism, in art and poetry, in 'many obscure and yet contested facts, now arranged under the name of Animal Magnetism; prayer; eloquence; self-healing; and the wisdom of children,' will become steady and habitual when the work of culture is complete, and 'you conform your life to the pure idea in your mind.' Then will come about, intellectually and practically, the kingdom of man that, to the eye of Reason, is no mythological prophecy sung by a poet to beguile the understanding into faith, but is now.

The full revolutionary force of what Emerson in these later chapters is saying is obscured by his Platonic and moralistic language, even in the exposition of his least orthodox thoughts. He himself, perhaps, does not fully appreciate the newness of what he is trying to say and wavers ambiguously between transcendental egoism and Platonic idealism. His originality remains impressive. One cannot demonstrate any important influence of Fichte or of any other source of German idealism on Emerson, although hints and echoes of this way of thinking were of course in the air. Though presumably he would not have moved in this direction if he had not been prompted to do so by some indirect Germanic influences, he still comes to this faith independently,

his will to believe such doctrine allowing him, without altogether understanding his own thought, to expand a few imperfect hints into a whole world-view.

His contemporary Theodore Parker knows little of this egoism, nor Hedge, nor Ripley, all three good German scholars;
the two latter cling to what vestiges of historical faith their
Unitarianism and intuitionism together may leave them; the
former is simply an intuitionary *philosophe,* deploying all his
scholarship in support of his grand design to try the creeds of
the churches and the constitutions of the states by the nature of
mankind and the constitution of the universe. Brownson again,
even at his most transcendental, has a social consciousness quite
foreign to this self-centeredness. Nor is there anything really
similar in Alcott's high-souled talk of Lapse and Birth and
Personalism, nor in Margaret Fuller's enthusiasms, nor even in
Thoreau, whose sensuous and spiritual self-immersion in nature
is quite unlike Emerson's desire to put nature under his feet.

Though Coleridge more than anyone else helped him to this
faith, his own religious experience and feeling is very different.
Perhaps Carlyle, heavily influenced by Fichte, provides the
closest parallel, but even he sees a call to duty and discipline
and *Entsagen* where Emerson, for all his moralism, sees the
emancipation of man. Borrowing hints and phrases from all
around him, responding with his uncanny sense for the key
thought to the intricate cross-influences of his time, Emerson yet
strikes one of the most startlingly new notes, all circumstances
considered, ever to be struck in American literature, while hardly
appearing to be aware that he has said anything unusual. The
lesson he would drive home is man's entire independence. The
aim of this strain in his thought is not virtue, but freedom and
mastery. It is radically anarchic, overthrowing all the authority
of the past, all compromise or coöperation with others, in the
name of the Power present and agent in the soul.

This revolutionary reading of his discovery of the God within,
as it is the most unsettling, so it is the most unstable. It could
come into being at all, one feels, only because of his peculiar
craving for self-dependence. And it is protected also by the

very fact that it is not the only element in Emerson's faith, but one member in an ambiguity. He could proclaim self-reliance because he could also advocate God-reliance; he could seek a natural freedom because he also sought a supernatural perfection; he could challenge society with his heresies because he considered himself closer to the true faith than they; he could assert that the individual is the world because, thanks to the moral law, we know that nothing arbitrary, nothing alien shall take place in the universe; the huge world, which he dared to defy, was really on his side and would not, as it were, spoil his game. The dual necessity, at once divergent and identical, to be free and invulnerable shapes much of his thinking.

We are now in a position to chart, not too seriously, the controlling geography of Emerson's mind. His favorite image of a polarity is inescapable here, for the rationale of fluid, poetic thinking like this, which affirms without thought of consistency the truth of the present insight, must be dynamic rather than systematic, a statement of the controlling opposites between which, by some organic law of undulation, his mental life swung. It is only the avoidance of a tight little dogma, the preservation of its negative capability, that makes such a mind interesting, and the student must be careful, as the hostile critic conspicuously is not, to avoid in his turn reducing him to easy formulas.

I propose, as a rude scaffolding for this analysis, the sufficiently difficult image of two crossed polarities. The north and south poles, the major axis, are the conceptual poles of the One and the Many, the Universal and the Individual, faith and the rest of experience, Reason and Understanding, between which Emerson saw man suspended. And across this lies a minor axis, whose poles, shifting and blending into each other, are harder to define, the temperamental west and east poles of pride and humility, egoism and pantheism, activity and passivity, Power and Law, between which, again, Emerson's nature was divided. Most of his central convictions can be plotted in some manner in relation to such coördinates. At the top of the chart belong the quasi-mystical moments in which, as he put it, he is dissolved in the Mind; self-reliance is a northwest idea; the moral law lies northeast; what Santayana called 'normal madness,' and Emerson 'exaggeration,' is southwest in quality; the idea of fate, perhaps, southeast.

The game is easy and not very profitable, nor do I hold any brief for the number or definition of these coördinates; yet they have a certain value. Chiefly I would stress the analogy of a polar field. As with Whitman, Melville, and Henry Adams, we are dealing with a mind that makes any assertion of belief against the felt pull of its lurking opposite, the two forming together a total *truth of experience* larger than the opposing *truths of statement* of which it is composed. Such a mind of course has 'double vision,' but it has a unity, too, though the unity of the poet's world rather than of the philosopher's system—the organic unity of the whole field as it is successively explored in thought. Only as we feel behind Emerson's rapt affirmations of the Soul, for example, the world of practical fact, which they deny *because it is also true*, can we gauge the quality of his thought. In the same way the vigor with which he insists today on freedom derives in part from his anticipation of the vigor with which tomorrow he will insist on law.

'Be yourself.' 'Be genuine.' 'My life is a May game, I will live as I like.' 'I would write on the lintels of the door-post, *Whim.*' Such declarations of unconditional independence best express the deepest drive of his nature, a drive he felt was sanctioned by the discovery of his proper deity. Yet his egoistic rebellion in the 1830's could not have announced, as did Whitman's,

> I harbor for good or bad, I permit to speak at every hazard,
> Nature without check with original energy.

'Be yourself' meant to Emerson 'Be your potential self.' The old longing for a change of nature, prompted by the early clash of his exorbitant ambition and his incapacity, was only intensified by his discovery that the grace and power of God, from which he had been taught to expect a rebirth to spring, was part of

parcel of his own soul by nature. The principle on which he set
out to base his life—'Live from within'—was not a means of
carefree liberation, but of strenuous and radical self-renewal.

We feel, then, for all the release they hail, a continuing
tension stiffening his journals and lectures of the period. To be
a 'true and free man' was a challenging, a heroic undertaking.
'The air . . . invites man with provoking indifference to total
indolence and to immortal actions. . . . the vast Eternity of
capacity, of freedom, opens before you, but without a single
impulse. . . . It demands something godlike in him who has cast
off the common yokes and motives of humanity, and has ven-
tured to trust himself for a taskmaster. High be his heart, faithful his will, vast his contemplations, that he may truly be a
world, society, law to himself; that a simple purpose may be to
him as strong as iron necessity is to others.' Generally, as was
his habit when under pressure, the effort received moralistic
formulation, particularly in the first years after he left the
Second Church. '. . . to govern my passions with absolute sway
is the work I have to do,' he wrote in 1831, and repeatedly his
language later is reminiscent of this Unitarian aspiration,
through rectitude, to 'Likeness to God.'

Yet his true goal was not really a Stoic self-mastery, nor
Christian holiness, but rather something more secular and harder
to define—a quality he sometimes called *entirety*, or *self-union*.
His aim, in Thoreau's terms, was to live deliberately, to seize
the nick of time. The common experience of life, for him as for
us, was of a succession of occasions, routine or unexpected, that
overtook the individual like the scenes that follow one another
outside the window of a moving train. The initiative lay with
what he called 'the exterior life,' the twin deities of Time and
Chance; the individual adapted himself to them as best he could,
in an eternal improvisation, formlessly strewn with half-for-
gotten themes and abandoned developments. To Emerson, as to
Thoreau, this was superficial and unnecessary. The individual
should somehow dominate his destiny, live so entirely from
within himself that he, as it were, initiated each new occasion
as it arrived. Only then, no longer 'drunk with the opium of

Time and Custom,' would he, as he once put it, ascend above his fate and work down upon his world.

This self-sufficient unity or wholeness, transforming his relations with the world about him, is, as I read him, the central objective of the egoistic or transcendental Emerson, the prophet of Man created in the 1830's by his discovery of the extent of his own proper nature. This was what he meant by 'sovereignty,' or 'mastery,' or the striking phrase, several times repeated, 'the erect position.' To enter for good the sanctuary of a free and absolute self-direction, such as he glimpsed in creative moments of insight and enthusiasm, was then his consuming ambition. 'We are very near to greatness: one step and we are safe: can we not take the leap?'

To take the leap into greatness he had to overcome two radical difficulties: the inconsecutiveness of his own moods, the impossibility of preserving the moments in which he felt his unity with the power within him; and the necessity of dealing with an outside world that remained obdurately independent of his will. The latter problem, deeply involved with his own continuing sense of community with and obligation to the world of men around him, I shall take up in the rest of this chapter and the first of the next, and then I shall turn to the former and even more crucial question.

'Society is, as men of the world have always found it, tumultuous, insecure, unprincipled. Society is cajoled and cowed and betrayed. . . . Society must come again under the yoke of the base and selfish but the individual heart faithful to itself is fenced with a sacred Palisado not to be traversed or approached unto, and is free forevermore.' The opposite and enemy of the sovereign self, as Emerson recognized in 'Self-Reliance,' is the community. The voice of cherub scorn for society that speaks in the above lecture of 1837 could be matched or exceeded by many similar passages dating from about that time. The shock of the 1837 depression, in particular, seems to have moved him to an open defiance. Himself sheltered from the worst of the blast, as it turned out, he responded to the stir in the air with a kind of holy joy. 'I see a good in such emphatic and universal calamity as the times bring[:] That they dissatisfy me with society. . . . Behold the boasted world has come to nothing. Prudence itself is at her wits' end.

'Pride, and Thrift, and Expediency, who jeered and chirped and were so well pleased with themselves, and made merry with the dream, as they termed it, of Philosophy and Love,—behold they are all flat, and here is the Soul erect and unconquered still. What answer is it now to say, It has always been so? . . . Let me begin anew; let me teach the finite to know its master. Let me ascend above my fate and work down upon my world.'

Phrases from this passage in his journal appear in the address he made, in Alcott's place, at the Greene St. School in Providence in the summer of 1837, and in the first lecture of his next winter's course on *Human Culture* he spoke out sharply and publicly against the tyranny of society.

Man, upright, reasoning, royal man, the master of the lower world, cannot be found, but instead—a deformed Society which confessedly does not aim at an ideal integrity, no longer believes it possible, and only aims by the aid of falsehoods at keeping down universal uproar, at keeping men from each other's throats. . . . A universal principle of compromise has crept into use. A Routine which no man made and for whose abuses no man holds himself accountable tyrannizes over the spontaneous will and character of all the individuals. . . . We are overpowered by this great Actual which, by the numbers, by the extent, by the antiquity lost in darkness of its arrangements, daunts our resolution and though condemned by the mind yet we look elsewhere in vain for a realized reform and we say, This is the way of the World, this is necessary, and we accept the yoke and accommodate our feet to the treadmill. . . .

[But] Before the steady gaze of the Soul, the whole life of man, the societies, laws, and property and pursuits of men, and the long procession of history, do blench and quail. Before this indomitable soul ever fresh and immortal the aged world owns its master. . . . And the clear perception of a single soul that somewhat universally allowed in society is wrong and rotten, is a prophecy as certain that sooner or later that thing will fall, as if all creatures arose and cried out, It shall end.

Although, in sounding this radical note, Emerson was certainly not alone—was, indeed, caught up in a rising wave of
social ferment in his region—in his case it had deep personal
roots. It grew from and continued the controversy he began
with his society—or, more accurately, with the idea or phantom
of society within himself—when he resigned his Boston charge.
His journals record a long struggle between his ingrained sense
of dependence on, and obligation to, society, and his stubborn
resolve at all costs to be his own master. His resignation, though
already stemming from this conflict, did not resolve it. On the
contrary, that single overt act of self-reliance, as it determined
the course of his outward life, so it had long repercussions in
the recesses of his own mind. Not until 1842, at least, ten years
after his apostasy, could he be said to have achieved a real inner
equilibrium; and it is possible to argue that not until the flatter-
ing invitations that resulted in his second trip to England in
1847-48, and that busy tour itself, had demonstrated to him
beyond doubt that he *had* achieved a leading position in society,
was he able at last to rest from his old anxiety.

His rebellion against the dominion of society encountered
two main inner obstacles: his fear of solitude, and his sense of
responsibility.

Balancing his centrifugal drive is a centripetal one, a craving
for unanimity and affection. As John Bard McNulty has brought
out, there is a latent warmth of humanity, and a concealed reference to many actual passages of friendship, beneath the surface
coldness of his essay 'Friendship,' for all its austere conclusion
that we walk alone in the world. So, after transcribing his essay
'Love' for the printer, Emerson confessed its inadequateness.
'I, cold because I am hot,—cold at the surface only as a sort of
guard and compensation for the fluid tenderness of the core,—
have much more experience than I have written there, more
than I will, more than I can write.' Against Emerson's lofty
dismissal of the half-gods we must set his loyalty to the old
affections of family—his devotion to his brother Charles, to
Ellen Tucker, to his son Waldo, the long and loving compan-

ionship with 'mine Asia,'—all of which amply demonstrate his capacity for affection, at least within his own clan.

Beyond the family circle, however, his craving for friendship and love seldom found adequate satisfaction. His relations with Alcott, with Carlyle, with Caroline Sturgis, let alone Thoreau or Margaret Fuller, were all disappointing at last, and he could only conclude sadly, 'Baulked soul! . . . Man is insular and cannot be touched.' For all the fluid tenderness at the core, invisible repulsions usually constrained him to awkwardness and aloofness with other men and denied his wish for companionship adequate overt expression, until by revulsion he felt like the transparently anonymous humorist in 'Society and Solitude' who, as he quotes him, is 'only waiting to shuffle off my corporeal jacket to slip away into the back stars, and put diameters of the solar system and sidereal orbits between me and all souls. . . .'

But the love at the heart, checked in one place, broke out elsewhere. For human relations Emerson substitutes ideal relations. The essay 'Friendship,' for example, in the end paints an ideal of friendship scarcely any human relation could realize and can end only with the 'sublime hope . . . that elsewhere, in other regions of the universal power, souls are now acting, enduring and daring, which can love us and which we can love.' So the essay 'Love,' for all its initial deification of persons, teaches, as the conclusion of 'Friendship' put it, 'True love transcends the unworthy object and dwells and broods on the eternal. . . .' The pattern these essays obey is habitual to Emerson. From the particular, the personal, the actual, he moves to the general, the impersonal, the ideal; the love unsatisfied on the level of persons is devoted to thoughts.

The Emerson the world encountered was therefore usually half and the lesser half of the man. Apart from men he lived an intense emotional life they could seldom see or share, except as he brought its fruits to them in his lectures and essays, or as they obscurely felt its aura surrounding his uncompanionable presence. Yet he also felt, often acutely, that such solitude, rich though it was, still cut him off from reality, was even not real living at all. Beside the life of thought in which he was at home was another life of association with other men from which he was debarred. A proper life would unite the two, but in his experience they were antithetical. *The American Scholar,* for example, written to demonstrate the social importance of 'Man Thinking,' betrays in its praise of action an underlying dissatisfaction with the scholar's life of solitary thought. 'I run eagerly into this resounding tumult. I grasp the hands of those next me, and take my place in the ring to suffer and to work. . . .' Unless the scholar acts, he wrote in 'Literary Ethics,' he is 'incomplete, pedantic, useless, ghostly.' Recurrently Emerson felt the loss of reality inherent in his detachment and repudiated his ghostly life for one in contact with real men.

But his wish for independence clashed also with his sense of obligation to be useful to the society he repudiated. He was not merely, by vocation, a sauntering poet, but a teacher, with grave social responsibilities to discharge. After leaving the ministry, for all the welcome he gave his promised freedom, he was deeply disturbed at the threatened loss of a recognized place among his fellows, and balanced his acknowledgment of his organic solitude with repeated attempts to demonstrate to his own satisfaction that, for all that he obeyed only his instincts, he still possessed an organic relation to society and was not an outcast or egotist, shirking his responsibilities in some private palace of art.

This concern was the price he paid for rejecting an established vocation, a rebellion that left him, even in his own eyes, without an evident place in New England life and so called into question the basis of his self-respect. A man's life could fairly be judged, he agreed, by the answer he was able to give to the question, 'Where is the fruit?' If by 1844 he thought he had learned to find a private fruit sufficient, less than seven years before he still felt a demand for an overt effect, a life of active usefulness.

This sense of an obligation to serve, clashing with his wish for freedom, generated characteristically a preoccupation with

'great action.' A life in union with the Soul would flood him
with a power of heroic performance that would sweep him and
his society together along new paths. His inner freedom, he
felt, could be guaranteed only by outward capacity. The duality
of his life did not then, as it did later, seem to lie between a
busybody activity and a passive worship of Ideas, but between a
habitual existence as a 'surprised spectator and learner' and
inspired moments in which, in his phrase, 'I am a Doer.' His
imagination became filled with images of past doers—Napoleon, for example, fascinated him—and with various large-scale
abstract character-types—The Reformer, The Scholar, The Hero
—shadowy outlines of the possible great emancipating roles he
felt he had it in him to play, with God his prompter. Gazing
into the magic mirror of his intuition, Emerson beheld Man in
his native power, a great responsible Thinker and Actor, whose
'victorious thought' one after another 'comes up with and re-
duces all things, until the world becomes at last only a realized
will,—the double of the man.'

   No task so caught Emerson's imagination as that of drawing
the portrait of the great man. He ransacked the pages of history
for examples of greatness and devoted an early lecture series,
and eventually a book, to the characters of great men. The example of the heroes and leaders of the past gave some color of
actuality to his vision of great action. 'In a century, in a millennium, one or two men; that is to say, one or two approximations
to the right state of every man. . . . Each philosopher, each bard,
each actor has only done for me, as by a delegate, what one
day I can do for myself.' The use of great men was to reveal us
to ourselves. 'We wish to hold these fellow minds as mirrors
before ourselves to learn the deepest secret of our capacity.'
'Then I dare; I also will essay to be.'
   One quality they all shared was force. The great man 'is
effective, generative; . . . he is constructive, fertile, magnetic. . . .'
He has tapped the springs of power. This is a quality shared by
all the great, that makes them such, whatever the particular
variety of possible greatness they illustrate; they are primary

or affirmative men. In his early lecture series on *Biography* Emerson flatly ascribes this force to the moral sentiment. Luther is great, for example, because 'He achieved a Spiritual revolution by spiritual arms alone,' by a 'sublime reliance on the simple force of truth.' So the lecture on Fox, the most personal of the five, portrays a man who, trusting wholly to the religious sentiment, outstripped the gifted, the cultivated, and the powerful and shook, by virtue of 'this enormous assertion of spiritual right, all the tyrannies, all the hierarchies, all the artificial ranks of the world.' It is an early sketch of the American scholar.

Yet he could not entirely overlook the evident distinction between the religious sentiment and the power to act. The moral sentiment could certainly inspire, but to conquer and prevail took more than ecstasy. To be a doer demands the knack, or character, or magnetism, or whatever personal force it is that gives one man ascendancy over another. Rationalized here and elsewhere as moral supremacy, in the end it could seem to him simply an arbitrary gift of destiny.

> I hold it of little matter
> Whether your jewel be of pure water,
>
> .   .   .   .   .   .
>
> But whether it dazzle me with light.

In his reflections on heroism we find his clearest recognition of the unsanctified aspect of practical power.

In a review in 1850 of *Representative Men,* Émile Montégut defined Emerson's idea of greatness as *antique,* a celebration of the great soul by nature, and rejected this easy greatness in favor of the Christian ideal of greatness by achievement and suffering, like that of Christ, an ideal he believed he found in Carlyle's *Heroes and Hero Worship.* Whatever the justice of this comparison, there can be little question that the antique Roman was the original model of Emerson's natural hero. The 'Doctor and historian' of heroism was Plutarch. 'I must think we are more deeply indebted to him than to all the ancient writers. . . . A wild courage, a Stoicism not of the schools but of the blood, shines in every anecdote, and has given that book its immense fame.'

Emerson's clearest celebration of this antique Stoicism of the blood is his essay 'Heroism,' originally one of a diptych of lectures portraying respectively 'Heroism' and 'Holiness.' The subject of the second lecture was the saint, 'the state of man under the dominion of the moral sentiment.' 'The saint . . . is a man who, accustomed to revere the moral sentiment as a law, discriminates it in his thinking from his private self; cuts it off; puts it far from him; calls it by another name; and attributes to himself none of its infinite worthiness; but contrasts the animal tendencies in him, with this overpowering worth; and so, is divided; and calls one, God, and worships it, and calls the other, himself, and flouts it.' The hero, on the other hand, was 'a concentration and exaltation of the Individual.' Heroes 'have never discriminated between their *individual* and what philosophy denominates their *universal* nature. . . .' The hero is man active, not philosophical; he is will without thought. 'There is somewhat not philosophical in heroism; there is somewhat not holy in it; it seems not to know that other souls are of one texture with it; it has pride; it is the extreme of individual nature.' Thus the spiritual perception of the scholar is eliminated by definition from Emerson's portrait of the hero, which becomes in its very partiality a clearer picture of the active element in Emerson's ideal of greatness, provided we bear in mind Emerson's own reservation, that '[holiness] overlooks [heroism], and gives a more precise account of it.'

'. . . [man] is born into the state of war.' There is a certain ferocity in nature—Emerson mentions lock-jaw, hydrophobia, insanity, war, plague, cholera, and famine—which a man must withstand; and there is, more real to Emerson, a ferocity in society, too, toward its nonconformists, which a man worth his salt must face and defy. The saint transcends these evils through faith. But most men need something of the saint and something of the hero to see them through all the crises of their active life. For them a sufficient faith is a matter of a very few hours

in a lifetime; for the rest they must fall back on their own resources of character. The hero is one whose own resources are
all he needs.

His leading trait is an unshakable will. The opposition of
men will not turn him aside from his purposes; the hero judges
for himself. So he scorns all that men call prudence. Most men
lead lives of petty calculation and low aims, pursue worldly
prizes and creature comforts, dote on health, or wealth, or
reputation. The hero lives on a plane above all this, where
such practical discretion has no meaning. Heroism 'is a self-
trust which slights the restraints of prudence, in the plenitude
of its energy and power to repair the harms it may suffer.'
Emerson cannot make too sharp the distinction between the
heroic and the common life. 'There seems to be no interval between greatness and meanness. When the spirit is not master of
the world, then it is its dupe.'

Above all, heroism is power: the hero is master of the world.
He has the promptitude, the energy, the instinct of success that
allows him to set aside ordinary prudence and bend events to
his will. The ease and hilarity of the hero, of which Emerson
makes a particular point, is a symptom of his mastery; in an
Age of Reflection the hero 'feels and never reasons, and therefore is always right. . . .' Emerson had been reading a good deal
about Napoleon before he wrote this lecture, and his later essay
on that man of the world is his most extended tribute to those
attributes of greatness which were polar to his own.

Now these traits of the hero, and particularly his practical
mastery, bear no obvious or necessary relation to virtue. Though
the hero is a doer, it does not follow that he must be a do-
gooder. Napoleon, Emerson came to concede, was a great
man, but he never called him a good one. The hero's secret
impulse need not be virtuous, it need only be successful. Nevertheless, the instinctive act of faith by which he defines the hero
as the soldier of virtue is central to his idea of heroism: 'The
essence of greatness is the perception that virtue is enough.'
Generally, outside this essay, he does not make such a sharp distinction between heroism and holiness. The hero's impulse, he

usually holds, is in fact one with the moral sentiment; in the last analysis, 'an able man is nothing else than a good, free, vascular organization, whereinto the universal spirit freely flows. . . . The hero is great by means of the predominance of the universal nature. . . .' Beneath what we might call his 'good conduit' theory of heroism, however, we can see the sayer's envy of the doer's power. The Nietzschean Superman is already half-explicit in Emerson's hero.

It is evident, I would assume, that Emerson's whole dream of practical power through Self-reliance is just that—a dream. Through it he attempted to meet the pressures of his actual world by creating, in his mind, a heroic personality endowed with a supreme power before which they would vanish. The product and expression of his personal tensions, it is clearly less a genuine program of action than what he afterwards called it, a romance. Miraculously, as it seemed, the discovery of the God within opened a door of escape from the trap of mortality, and the imprisoned spirit rushed to pass through.

Meanwhile, life went on, and with it its mundane difficulties. While Emerson's greatness originates in the power of faith that turned him aside from the path of convention, he retains our respect for him as a man by his capacity to recognize the facts of his condition, even while most enraptured by his romance of infinitude. Through and under the vast claims of his faith runs a common-sense realistic perception of the actual state of affairs, as an intermittent recognition of the waking world offsets the prodigious dream of *Finnegans Wake*.

We see this, for example, in the way he both admired and contemned all that he called prudence. His common sense revolted at any foolish neglect of the practical conditions of life in the name of heroism. No one is exempt from the laws of life. Promptness, thrift, industry, forethought, temperance, courage are virtues for us all alike. It is all very well to be 'the helpful giant to destroy the old or to build the new,' if you can manage it; but imprudent genius dies 'exhausted and fruitless, like a giant slaughtered by pins.' A scrupulous attention to such things as health, bread, climate, and social position is the first practical condition of freedom, and an indispensable school of character. Common sense teaches that nothing great can be expected from a man who cannot learn to manage little things. And yet such prudence is unideal; it is the virtue of the senses. He could try, in such essays as 'Prudence,' to show how prudence and heroism could and should be reconciled, but one moment's renewed *experience* of the ideal was apt to shatter his case. The holy times of insight and moral sentiment were memorable partly because they seemed to raise him above the whole realm of being which made prudence necessary. Prudence was god of this world; but man was great and happy, Emerson's faith insisted, only as he set his foot on this world and lived in the spirit, above prudence.

Inescapably, common sense said, his was the bifold life of the scholar, part contemplation, part routine daily living. And yet his faith promised so much more! Its whole point and force was the revelation of a new life-principle which would redeem him from routine. To concede, with common sense, that life *must* be dual was as much as to concede the emptiness of the liberation his discovery of the omnipotence of the Soul had seemed to open to him, and was therefore something he came to slowly, partially, and with the utmost reluctance. If freedom lay only in the total self-trust of greatness, and if in fact he could be great only in inceptions and not in act, how did his new faith free him? The duality of his experience, condemning him to glimpses of a kingdom to which he was entitled by his constitution, yet which he could not enter, seemed to him at first a vanishing anomaly, then a wild and bewildering contradiction, and finally an absurdity of fate which he must learn to accept as best he might.

The enthusiastic vision of a rebirth into greatness, in the might of the God within, that would inaugurate a spiritual revolution in society also is thus the dynamic element in his early thought. As it takes hold, around 1833, the succession of his journal entries falls into an erratic alternating movement of aspiration and retreat, as fresh gusts of hope catch his imagination and then subside. A greatness that would conquer and prevail seemed to him at first his great opportunity and somehow his obligation; every man should 'live a life of discovery and performance.' Yet he also knew all the time that such ideas were simply an extravagance of faith, and that the scholar's life with which he was familiar would always be his fate. The chief problem he had to solve in these years was not so much how to achieve greatness, as how to bring his dream of great action into some kind of contact with facts and square it with experience.

CHAPTER FOUR

The Question of Means

TO BRING to the test of experience his vague but power-ful ambition to be a doer was the chief service performed for Emerson by the wave of social reform that arose in the late thirties and early forties in New England. The reformers called on him to perform exactly the kind of action he recognized a duty and claimed a potential capacity to perform—and when confronted with the actuality of his ambition, he discovered that it was something which he had no aptitude or wish to do, and which threatened the very liberation to which his faith had opened the way. As a consequence, the whole atmosphere of his faith underwent a pervasive change, as he adjusted his beliefs to protect the old values in the new situation. Not that the issue of reform alone caused this change. His original faith had been attuned to a millennialism which time and experience alone inevitably did much to weaken. In point of fact, we can see other contributing circumstances which increased the instability of his initial hopes, until the question of action forced on him by the reform movement precipitated their revision.

The kind of action Emerson understood best was that of the preacher. His proper role in society, he felt, was that inspired communication of truth which he called eloquence. '. . . it is the end of eloquence,' he held, 'in a half-hour's discourse,—perhaps by a few sentences,—to persuade a multitude of persons to renounce their opinions, and change the course of life.' This ambition was particularly strong in the early 1830's, while he still hoped sometime to replace his old church with a 'little chapel of the truth.' Then he imagined, 'The high prize of eloquence may be mine, the joy of uttering what no other can utter, and what all must receive'; and at moments he felt 'budding the powers of a Persuasion that by and by will be irresistible.' Here was a mode of greatness which he could

72

aspire to with some color of plausibility. 'If I could persuade men to listen to their interior convictions, if I could express, embody their interior convictions, that were indeed life. It were to cease being a figure, and to act the action of a man.'

There is some evidence that the Divinity School *Address* in 1838 was involved emotionally more than he knew with this personal sense of mission. It had perhaps the deepest roots in his thoughts of any of his lectures, being an exposition of the spiritual religion for the sake of which he had abandoned the pulpit. The substance of the address was explicit in the journals in 1833, and already by 1835 he had formed an intention to 'write & print a discourse upon Spiritual & Traditional Religion. . . .' The address came as close to the irresistible truth he felt called on to announce to his generation as any of his utterances. Had he not written, 'When anyone comes who speaks with better insight into moral nature, he will be the new gospel; miracle or not, inspired or uninspired, he will be the Christ . . .'?

He was correspondingly affected by its hostile reception. Though outwardly unruffled and even amused, inwardly he was definitely perturbed, as the repeated self-defenses in his journals show. The reception of his address was the sharpest hint yet given him from the actual that its limitations were not to be lightly ignored. Inherently a contradiction of fact, the faith in his potential mastery was constantly exposed to the erosion of experience, which daily reminded him that the mountains he had declared to be moving were still in place. The reception of the *Address* was an angular intrusion of fact into the smooth world of his thoughts, which, while rousing him to an unprecedented vigor of defiance, helped to undermine in the long run his capacity to identify the ideal and the real.

His sharpest immediate response was a renewed defiance of society. In the solitude of his study he rose in the insulted majesty of the Soul and prophesied against his critics.

. . . The world lies in night of sin. It hears not the cock crowing: it sees not the grey streak in the East. At the first entering ray 'of light, society is shaken with fear and anger from side to side. Who opened that shutter? they cry, Wo to him! They belie it, they call it darkness that comes in, affirming that they were in light before. Before the man who has spoken to them the dread word, they tremble and flee. . . . The wild horse has heard the whisper of the tamer: the maniac has caught the glance of the keeper. They try to forget the memory of the speaker, to put him down into the same obscure place he occupied in their minds before he spake to them. . . . But vain, vain, all vain. It was but the first mutter of the distant storm they heard,—it was the first cry of the Revolution,—it was the touch, the palpitation that goes before the earthquake. Even now society is shaken because a thought or two have been thrown into the midst. . . . It now works only in a handful. . . . But the doom of State Street, and Wall Street, of London, and France, of the whole world, is advertised by those thoughts; is in the procession of the Soul which comes after those few thoughts.

The passage is a magnificent eruption of the apocalyptic fire that smoldered in the heart of this son of the Puritans.

Yet he was stirred to this peak of aggressiveness partly by a certain shock to his confidence, as its whole context in the journals suggests. Some years later, he allegorically and ironically reviewed the affair in his poem 'Uriel,' for which the passage just quoted may well have been the germ. The stress in the poem falls on the two points I wish to bring out: the revolutionary nature of Uriel's utterance, and the lapse of Uriel himself that followed it.

The address itself was calculated to give no offense, on grounds of vocabulary at least, to a Unitarian audience. To compensate for the audacity of his purpose, perhaps, he instinctively emphasized the regularity and morality of the inner life with which he would replace external forms. That freedom, and not just a higher law, was the intent of the spiritual religion advocated in the Divinity School *Address* is made clear in 'Uriel.' There Uriel is not the discoverer of a new principle of order, but is subversive of all order.

> One, with low tones that decide,
>
> .   .   .   .
>
> Gave his sentiment divine
> Against the being of a line.

'Line in nature is not found,
Unit and universe are round,
In vain produced, all rays return,
Evil will bless, and ice will burn.'

True, the tone of the poem is ironical. Uriel is the deadly
child in the house who does not know better than to speak the
truth in company. The old war gods are right: such a menace
must be removed at once. Emerson ironically accepts the re-
spectable definition of good and evil and deliberately leaves
out of account the higher order which in fact he had advocated
to replace the false conventions of his society. But in so doing
he reveals what his address glossed over, his sharp consciousness that his gospel *was* disruptive of the actual social order.
Uriel is the enemy of all worldly authority, and one can read
between the lines that he delights in the confusion his treason
caused.

His lapse, in turn, is no repentance. The self-knowledge that
withers him is a knowledge of his impotence. Perhaps he is not
ready to speak, perhaps he is 'grown too bright,' but certainly
his society cannot bear to hear him; his hour is not ripe. He
stands outside his conventional society in the freedom and the
solitude of outer space. The most he can do is to shake its
security with occasional hints of his cherub scorn. The poem
thus involuntarily conveys the depth of Emerson's antipathy to
the community he challenged. Uriel's truth is allied to the in-
animate forces of nature, and its utterance, while it shakes
society, transforms him also into something fey and inhuman.
In this poem, as elsewhere in his writings, we touch the chilling
core of Emerson's idealism and sense the presence there of
something with which no community is possible.

In a life lived so entirely in the mind as his, every serious
engagement with the outer world had long-continued repercussions, as he gradually assimilated the implications of the
brute event into the tissue of his thought. His break with his
Boston church was such a key event, and so to a lesser extent
was the *Address*. It forced him to see that society did not *want*

to renounce their opinions for the truth. In *The American Scholar* Emerson had described a new Moses; 'Uriel' is the ironical allegory of such a Moses whose people preferred the desert. After this time Emerson's image of the hero-scholar, leading mankind to the promised land, steadily gave way to that of the solitary observer, unregarded and unregarding of the multitude, quietly faithful to his inspired glimpses of worlds not realized.

> Let theist, atheist, pantheist,
> Define and wrangle how they list,
> Fierce conserver, fierce destroyer,—
> But thou, joy-giver and enjoyer,
> Unknowing war, unknowing crime,
> Gentle Saadi, mind thy rhyme . . . .

The process thus assisted by the affair of the Divinity School *Address* was carried on and brought to a conclusion by the wave of reforming excitement that swept over certain elements in New England at the end of the fourth and the beginning of the fifth decade of the nineteenth century. As a phenomenon, Emerson welcomed and encouraged it. When impelled to ask, 'Is the ideal society always to be only a dream, a song, a luxury of thought, and never a step taken to realize the vision for living and indigent men without misgivings within and wildest ridicule abroad?' he could point to the reformer: 'I, for my part, am very well pleased to see the variety and velocity of the movements that all over our broad land, in spots and corners, agitate society. War, slavery, alcohol, animal food, domestic hired service, colleges, creeds, and now at last money, also, have their spirited and unweariable assailants, and must pass out of use or must learn a law.'

He acquired for a time a 'habitual feeling that the whole of our social structure—State, School, Religion, Marriage, Trade, Science—has been cut off from its root in the soul, and has only a superficial life, a "name to live." ' Reform became his name for whatever would allow him 'to restore for myself these fruits to their stock, or to accept no church, school, state, or society which did not found itself in my own nature. . . . I should like to put all my practices back on their first thoughts, and do nothing for which I had not the whole world for my reason.'

Yet the gap between dream and fact remained. He never undertook the leap of faith and avoided the heroic life in practice. In his discussion of reform, we can perceive an underlying consciousness, increasing with time, that the whole enterprise is essentially romance. Thus, side by side with his deep sympathy with reform as a general idea, we find a progressive disillusionment with all actual reforms. Typical of his feeling toward concrete schemes of reform is his refusal to join the Brook Farm community.

This refusal is superficially surprising, because the root idea of that transcendental asylum was the most attractive of all reforms to Emerson, the one he called the Doctrine of the Farm: the scholar should not live by thought alone but should put himself into primary relations with the soil and nature by performing his part in the manual labor of the world. This sensible suggestion that the sedentary intellectual should spend some of his time outdoors and take adequate exercise meant much more to Emerson. Most of all, it seemed to him a means of approaching that *entirety* in his own life and his outer relations which was his deepest desire. The doctrine expressed an ideal of self-sufficiency through simplicity. A man should scale his needs down to the point where he could meet them by his own exertions. Such an ideal, of course, could never be completely realized, but steps could be taken to draw closer to it, each one of which would free one that much more from living for show and bring one that much closer to the holy and mysterious recesses of life. *Walden* is the logical outcome of this way of thinking, and Thoreau's 'Simplify, simplify' its slogan. But this was also an aim of Brook Farm—to simplify life and restore its primary relations with the soil. *Walden* and Brook Farm are alternative means for attaining the end that Emerson formulated for both when he wrote, 'The power which is at once spring and regulator in all efforts of reform is the conviction that there is an infinite worthiness in man, which will appear at the call of worth, and that all particular reforms are the removing of some impediment.'

But if the aim of reform for Emerson was independence, we can understand why he decided not join the Brook Farmers, even though their aim was similar; for 'At the name of a society all my repulsions play, all my quills rise & sharpen.' 'I do not wish to remove from my present prison to a prison a little larger,' he wrote. 'I wish to break all prisons.' Ripley's project seemed a pretty circuitous route to the few, simple conditions he required. 'I have not yet conquered my own house. It irks and repents me. Shall I raise the siege of this hencoop, and march baffled away to a pretended siege of Babylon?' The only reform that mattered to him, after all, was moral and personal.

His objection to Brook Farm, he found, applied to all co-operative schemes of reform; they were all external. 'The Reformers affirm the inward life, but they do not trust it, but use outward and vulgar means.' They were partial in their aims, exhausting their efforts on some contemptible village or dog-hutch; they banded themselves together in associations or phil-anthropic societies, relying on numbers instead of themselves. In coming closer to such reform he did not hear the call of worth, but found himself 'jostled, crowded, cramped, halved, quartered, or on all sides diminished of his proportion'; and he swung back, with some violence, to the sanctuary of the heart. 'I cannot find language of sufficient energy to convey my sense of the sacredness of private integrity.'

He thus found forced on him an open repudiation of his supposed obligation to act. True, 'These reforms are . . . our own light, and sight, and conscience; they only name the relation which subsists between us and the vicious institutions which they go to rectify.' Yet no one of them but was partial and superficial. Plainly then, such manipular attempts to realize the world of thought were premature. 'Many eager persons successively make an experiment in this way, and make themselves ridiculous. . . . Worse, I observe that in the history of mankind there is never a solitary example of success,—taking their own tests of success.' Then perforce he must consent to inaction. Henry Nash Smith points out that when, in his lecture on 'The Times,' Emerson divides the movement party into the actors and the students, and rejects the former for the latter, he is formally repudiating the ideal of great action.

Yet the students are reformers too. Impressed, like the actors, with 'the contrast of the dwarfish Actual with the exorbitant Idea,' they see also that all practical effort to reduce this contrast is inadequate and are thus thrown back on beholding. 'It is not that men do not wish to act; they pine to be employed, but are paralyzed by the uncertainty what they should do.' One would suppose that such passive futility would earn Emerson's disapproval equally with the busy futility of the actors, and certainly he does not approve the students unreservedly. They do not show the natural firmness of a man, but a certain imbecility that is the result of their insoluble perplexities. Sicklied o'er with the pale cast of thought, their life is deprived of its natural spontaneity and joy and is oppressed with ennui and melancholy.

Yet Emerson values the students above the actors: 'Of the two, I own I like the speculators best.' The reason is, 'Their unbelief arises out of a greater Belief. . . .' Their aim and wish is to to give up entirely to the spiritual principle, and therefore they abstain from low methods of changing society, realizing that all higher modes of living and action must proceed from a prior renovation of the actor. 'Their fault is that they have stopped at the intellectual perception; that their will is not yet inspired from the Fountain of Love.' 'But whose fault is this?' Emerson asks. At least they understand what and where is the spring of all power. The student is sustained, however, like the actor, by a sense of his potential greatness and of an imminent revolution in society. He will keep in training, trim his lamp and wait. 'A patience which is grand; a brave and cold neglect of the offices which prudence exacts, so it be done in a deep upper piety; a consent to solitude and inaction which proceed out of an unwillingness to violate character, is the century which makes the gem.'

Emerson returned to the students and characterized them at greater length in his lecture 'The Transcendentalist,' fourth in the same series on *The Times.* This lecture, by the fact of its title, has acquired a factitious authority, as though it were a definitive statement of what Emerson and his movement-party friends were about. It does indeed tell us much about its creator and about his times, but it must be read against some such background as I have tried to sketch in to be fully understood. In this case, he is clearly describing a *second choice*. Since the ideal of the scholar, who does live in the soul and lead men like a hero, has increasingly come to seem unrealizable, Emerson describes instead the closest practical substitute—a scholar on the waiting list, so to speak. He repeatedly makes it clear that his highest praise is reserved, as before, for strong spirits, for heroes. The transcendentalist is only the negative half of a man; he is an empty cup, but at least the cup is ready for filling.

The lack of spontaneity in the character of the transcendentalist soon disaffected Emerson with him also. Somehow his faith in greatness had led him into a blind alley. 'If we suddenly plant our foot and say,—I will neither eat nor drink nor wear nor touch any food or fabric which I do not know to be innocent, or deal with any person whose whole manner of life is not clear and rational, we shall stand still.' It is reasonable to rebel against one bad custom, as did the reformers, but the effort to uproot *all* custom from our life can end only in emptying it of everything except the paralyzing custom of saying No.

At this point we are ready to pay attention to the case of the Conservative, to whom Emerson devoted a lecture in the same series that included 'The Transcendentalist.' Though included, perhaps, as Burke seems to have been included in the series on *Biography,* for proper variety, he is portrayed with considerable sympathy. The conservative is one who respects facts—as Emerson was learning to do. His fault is that he has no faith; he also is a half-man. Yet his partial statement is within its limits indisputable and is something the reformer ignores at his peril.

That which is best about conservatism . . . is the Inevitable. . . . Here is the fact which men call Fate, and fate in dread degrees, fate behind fate, not to be disposed of by the consideration that the Conscience commands this or that, but necessitating the question whether the faculties of man will play him true in resisting the facts of universal experience? . . . We have all a certain intellection or presentiment of reform existing in the mind, which does not yet descend into the character, and those who throw themselves blindly on this lose themselves. Whatever they attempt in that direction, fails, and reacts suicidally on the actor himself. This is the penalty of having transcended nature. For the existing world is not a dream, and cannot with impunity be treated as a dream; neither is it a disease; but it is the ground on which you stand, it is the mother of whom you were born. Reform converses with possibilities, perchance with impossibilities; but here is sacred fact.

Though Emerson in the end still affirms his allegiance to the movement party, he treats the reformer in this lecture as a half-man, too. Each is an example of the exaggerating propensities of man, who cannot be a whole, but seizes on a half-truth and pursues it beyond all proportion. In the person of his conservative, a forerunner of his skeptic,[1] Emerson takes a long step away from his earlier commitment to the movement party, toward a greater disengagement and a more balanced recognition of the permanent part played in life by both idea and fact. Other lectures of this pivotal course reflect the same step to a lesser degree.

Emerson's answer to a heroic declaration of Alcott's, some five years later, shortly after the latter, with his English friends Lane and Wright, and their 'twelve manuscript volumes of J. P. Greaves, and his head in a plaster cast,' had failed with their scheme for a 'Concordium' at Fruitlands, was by then his answer to every transcendental reformer, including the one in himself. 'Alcott thought he could find as good a ground for

[1] See Chapter 6.

quarrel in the state tax as Socrates did in the edict of the Judges.
Then I say, Be consistent. . . . Say boldly, "There is a sword
sharp enough to cut sheer between flesh and spirit, and I will
use it, and not any longer belong to this double-faced, equivo-
cating, mixed, Jesuitical universe."

'. . . Your objection, then, to the State of Massachusetts is
deceptive. Your true quarrel is with the state of Man.' Very
neat, very well put, we can agree; but we may put to Emerson
his own later question to Webster, *How came he there?* What
else had the transcendentalist ever objected to than the state
of Man? A new scepticism controls this comment on Alcott's
anarchistic objection to the State which might well have disconcerted that good man, who had only to turn to Emerson's
recently printed essay on 'Politics' to find objections to the
states of Man and Massachusetts very similar to his own. But
that essay was based on a lecture given in 1837, with additions
from another of 1840, and since then Emerson had been
visited by many second thoughts.

Emerson's farewell to action is finally as explicit as his earlier
rejection of society, and for much the same reasons: his freedom
was threatened. 'Do not ask me to your philanthropies, charities,
and duties, as you term them;—mere circumstances, flakes of the
snow-cloud, leaves of the trees;—I sit at home with the cause,
grim or glad. I think I may never do anything that you shall call
a deed again.' The conclusion of the essay 'Spiritual Laws,' in
particular, is a rapid barrage of arguments against the name of
action, most of them dating from the same year as the passage
just quoted. '. . . why should we be cowed by the name of
Action? 'T is a trick of the senses,—no more. We know that
the ancestor of every action is a thought.' '. . . real action,' this
essay argues, 'is in silent moments,' in the silent thought that
revises our entire manner of life. He stated what he was getting
at most plainly in 1845. 'The near-sighted people have much to
say about action. But . . . It is by no means action which is the
essential point, but some middle quality indifferent both to poet
and to actor, and which we call Reality.'

He had already in at least one passage come to the same point from the opposite direction in *The American Scholar,* when disillusioned with the partiality of thought, as he is in 'Spiritual Laws' with that of action. '. . . when thoughts are no longer apprehended,' he then argued, '. . . [the scholar] has always the resource *to live.* . . . This is a total act. Thinking is a partial act. . . . Time shall teach him that the scholar loses no hour which the man lives.'

Against this background we can understand his increasing admiration for what he called Character. This 'elemental force,' —'a certain solidity of merit, . . . which is so essentially and manifestly virtue, that it is taken for granted that the right . . . step will be taken by it'—a combination of probity and practical competence in coöperation with, rather than in defiance of, the order of society—which in *The American Scholar* Emerson had found higher than intellect, became more and more his practical ideal, as his hope of a life of discovery and performance died out. His realization of the futility of reform correspondingly increased his valuation of this 'reserved force, which acts directly by presence and without means,' until, in his second series of essays, he went so far as to look to it for a 'victory to the senses' that would eclipse the 'great defeat' of Christ on the cross! But this attractive idea of action by magnetism does not solve his problem; it only lays bare the heart of it: How is such private quality bred?

Beneath the question of action lay a deeper problem, that of man's compound nature. This was the question that most seriously concerned the transcendentalists, beside which society's criticism of their inaction was superficial. '. . . the two lives, of the understanding and of the soul, which we lead, really show very little relation to each other; . . . one prevails now, all buzz and din; and the other prevails then, all infinitude and paradise.' 'The object of the man,' he wrote elsewhere, 'the aim of these moments [of silent thought], is to make daylight shine through him, to suffer the law to traverse his whole being without obstruction. . . . Now he is not homogeneous, but heterogeneous, and the ray does not traverse. . . .' Even if we drop the question

of action, and seek only 'Reality,' the problem still remains,
How is such wholeness to be won and kept? Is there any ground
for hope 'that the moments will characterize the days'?

❧

The means to this wholeness was what Emerson called Culture, a topic to which he devoted a lecture series in 1837-38.
'His own Culture,—the unfolding of his nature, is the chief end
of man,' he told his audience. 'A divine impulse at the core of
his being, impels him to this. The only motive at all commensurate with his force, is the ambition to discover *by exercising* his latent power. . . .' The single man, ideally the master of
the world, is actually its pupil. No little part of Emerson's
journals and other writings, particularly around this time,
amount to an extended inventory of the educational facilities
open to him.

Culture is a term that one associates more with his later
thought than with the years of transcendental protest. He devoted an essay to it in *The Conduct of Life;* a Phi Beta Kappa
address in 1867 at Harvard treated 'The Progress of Culture';
his essay on Goethe in *Representative Men* also discussed it. In
these cases it signified chiefly all the influences that went to refine
and redeem the raw egoism of the natural man. In the 1830's,
however, when he had just picked up this 'Germanic term,' it
meant rather the means that would release the wild nature of a
man and redeem him from custom and tradition. 'Culture, in
the high sense, does not consist in polishing or varnishing, but in
so presenting the attractions of nature that the slumbering attributes of man may burst their iron sleep and rush, full-grown,
into day.' It was a method of conversion, and its goal the kind
of supernatural primitivism celebrated in the Divinity School
Address, the awakening of the Soul. 'To coax and woo the strong
Instinct to bestir itself and work its miracle is the end of all wise
endeavor.'

By rights, Emerson felt, man should enter at a bound into his
proper nature, annihilating his lower life by one blow of moral
revolution. The bent spring, released, should snap upright by its

own strength. But what were the means of release? The soul has various faculties, particularly the reason and the will; through which is its redemption to be achieved? Emerson did not know and at different times conceded primacy to each. The question to which he devoted much of his thought, especially in the decade or so after 1833, was that of the means of both moral and intellectual culture—the purification of the heart and the inspiration of the mind.

At the outset, he appears to have hoped for much from a course of ascetic self-discipline. Natural goodness was to be bred by a stern, high, stoical self-denial. 'I believe that virtue purges the eye, that the abstinent, meek, benevolent, industrious man is in a better state for the fine influences of the great universe to act upon him than the cold, idle, eating disputant.' So the paragraph in *Nature* containing the revelation that man is himself the creator in the finite concludes, 'This view, which admonishes me where the sources of wisdom and power lie, and points to virtue as to

> The golden key
> Which opes the palace of eternity,

carries upon its face the highest certificate of truth, because it animates me to create my own world through the purification of my soul.' The same preparatory asceticism is expounded in his address 'Literary Ethics,' where for discipline he recommends to the scholar solitude, labor, modesty and charity. '. . . we have need of a more rigorous scholastic rule; such an asceticism, I mean, as only the hardihood and devotion of the scholar himself can enforce. . . . Silence, seclusion, austerity, may pierce deep into the grandeur and secret of our being, and so diving, bring up out of secular darkness the sublimities of the moral constitution.' 'If [the scholar] have this twofold goodness,—the drill and the inspiration,—then he has health. . . .'

As it turned out, however, the drill and the inspiration had little relation to each other; health remained an unpredictable miracle. For this reason the theme of preparatory asceticism in time virtually dropped out of his thought; it simply did not work. The ethical life he knew was necessarily divided between moments of inspiration, and long intermediary times in which all his obedience to duty brought little visible fruit.

Duty he obeyed, nevertheless—for this was a primary obligation, whatever his state of grace. 'If we cannot at once rise to the sanctities of obedience and faith,' he wrote, 'let us at least resist our temptations. . . .' 'It is very hard to know what to do if you have great desires for benefitting mankind; but a very plain thing is your duty.' In the anomalous life of delay and waiting to which he was generally condemned, adrift in time and mortality, the one sea-anchor was the old elementary moral code he had learned in childhood. 'Play out the game,' he wrote his friends in later life. 'If the Gods have blundered, we will not.' 'We are thrown back on rectitude forever and ever, only rectitude,—to mend one; that is all we can do.'

Intellectual culture looked more promising. Here, he found, 'The means of culture is the related nature of man.' The same outside world from which culture was to wean the soul was also in all its parts a means to culture. '[Man] is so strangely related to every thing that he can go nowhere without meeting objects which solicit his senses, and yield him new meanings.' 'Let none wrong the truth,' he reminded himself, 'by too stiffly standing on the cold and proud doctrine of self-sufficiency.' '. . . nothing but God is self-dependent. Man is powerful only by the multitude of his affinities.' Since the NOT ME is, in the phrase from *The American Scholar*, a 'shadow of the soul, or *other me*,' man may confidently turn to it to find the means to awaken the 'me of me.'

The simplest way to distinguish between Emerson's rebellion against the outside world and his reliance on it for culture is to point out that in the former case he was thinking primarily of organized society, and in the latter primarily of nature. There is no question that nature could on occasion prompt the strong instinct to work its miracle. Several moments of sacred exhilaration are recorded in *Nature*, of which the 'transparent eyeball' passage is the most famous. Emerson's moments of gladness in nature, however, like Wordsworth's, diminished in number and intensity as he grew older. He soon came to see, also, that '. . . it is certain that the power to produce this delight does not reside in nature, but in man, or in a harmony of both.' Nature was at most 'a differential thermometer detecting the presence or absence of the divine spirit in man.' The illusion which he cherished in 1836 of a possible divine rapture to grow out of his wild poetic delight in nature had vanished by 1844. 'That bread which we ask of Nature is that she should entrance us, but amidst her beautiful or her grandest pictures I cannot escape the *second thought*. . . .'

But in the earlier period he entertained a more specific hope from nature which appears in the chapter of *Nature* on 'Language.' Nature was not merely a tonic to the spirit; she was significant of herself and spoke to the intelligence. Newly severed from the authority of the Bible, this reminiscent Puritan sought to read a new gospel from nature, God's perpetual revelation. 'Nature is a language, and every new fact that we learn is a new word; but rightly seen, taken all together, it is not merely a language, but the language put together into a most significant and universal book. I wish to learn the language, not that I may learn a new set of nouns and verbs, but that I may read the great book which is written in that tongue.'

For a brief while Emerson was attracted to Emanuel Swedenborg and his followers as interpreters of the language of nature. The influence of the Swedenborgians on his thought started with his reading of Sampson Reed's *The Growth of the Mind* in 1826 and reached its high point about ten years later. *Nature* contains numerous Swedenborgian echoes, more by a good margin than any subsequent writing of Emerson's. After that time he became increasingly conscious of Swedenborg's limitations—there is a distinct cooling off apparent between the paragraph on Swedenborg in *The American Scholar* and the essay on Swedenborg in *Representative Men*—at the same time that the New Church men in New England began publicly to repudiate him and the transcendentalism he represented.

What drew him was clearly the doctrine of correspondence.

Swedenborg developed this as a method of interpreting Scripture, but it was easily susceptible of a poetic extension, and that by warrant of the master: 'The whole natural world corresponds to the spiritual world, and not merely the natural world in general, but also every particular of it; and as a consequence every thing in the natural world that springs from the spiritual world is called a correspondent. . . . The animals of the earth correspond in general to affection, mild and useful animals to good affections, fierce and useless ones to evil affections. In particular, cattle and their young correspond to the affections of the natural mind, sheep and lambs to the affections of the spiritual mind; while birds correspond, according to their species, to the intellectual things of the natural mind or the spiritual mind,' etc., etc. Emerson easily took the short step from this notion of a fixed natural symbolism to the conclusion that nature is not only a language but a book, that spiritual truths may be read directly from nature, by a purged mind, without the intervention of any other revelation. Hence, 'All things . . . preach to us.'

However congenial the thought of a mute gospel in nature to his truth-hungry mind, he quickly exhausted the Swedenborgians. Already in 1835 he was writing to Elizabeth Peabody, 'I sympathize with what you say of your aversion at being confined to Swedenborg's associations. . . .' The literalism of Swedenborg became one of his main points of criticism in *Representative Men*. 'The slippery Proteus is not so easily caught. In nature, each individual symbol plays innumerable parts, as each particle of matter circulates in turn through every system. . . . Nature avenges herself speedily on the hard pedantry that would chain her waves. She is no literalist.' He soon dropped the notion that the meanings of natural objects could ever be fixed and written down. Yet a general sense that somewhere, beneath the surfaces of nature, lurked some great final meaning, if he could only get at it, continued to tease his reflections on nature. 'The love of Nature,—what is that but the presentiment of intelligence of it? Nature preparing to become a language to us.'

A more far-reaching attack on the meaning of nature was through natural science. Emerson shared the lively interest in the findings of science of his time, particularly in the emerging studies of geology and biology, but his spirit was hardly scientific. He read the ordinary fare available to the general reader of the day: J. F. W. Herschel, Cuvier, Humboldt, Playfair and later Lyell on geology, Kirby and Spence's *Entomology* and other such texts, various volumes in popular collections such as the *Library of Useful Knowledge, The American Library of Useful Knowledge,* Lardner's *The Cabinet Cyclopaedia,* several of the Bridgewater treatises, not to speak of browsings in the *Transactions of the Royal Society* and other periodical literature. Scientists like Galileo, Newton, Laplace, Lamarck, Linnaeus, Davy, Euler were high in his extensive list of great names.

What did he read this literature for? In the somewhat desultory years just after his return from Europe, when he did much such reading and lectured several times to groups of amateur students of science like himself, he more than once asked himself that question and finally confessed that he did not entirely know. '. . . all the reasons seem to me to fall far short of my faith upon the subject. Therefore, boldly press the cause as its own evidence; say that you love Nature, and would know her mysteries, and that you believe in your power by patient contemplation and docile experiment to learn them.' He read what the scientists had to say because he hoped to find in them some clue to nature's meanings.

Much of the writing on science that came to his hand was more or less apologetic in character, the Bridgewater treatises being an extreme example, anxious to protect science against the charge of atheism and encouraging a habit of sifting the scientific facts for evidences of divine contrivance. In this semipious atmosphere it was easy for Emerson to treat science, as he did, as a kind of embryonic revelation. His key thought on science was what he called, prompted by Coleridge, the 'humanity of science.' Nature was the 'externization' of something deep in man's consciousness; therefore man had somewhere within him the means of understanding all the phenomena of nature. True science was then as much a matter of extracting from oneself the Idea of the phenomena one knew as of collecting facts to be understood; find the true principles of unity in things, and the more or less of mere facts becomes unimportant. Since Goethe's scientific accomplishment, genetic and anti-Newtonian student of nature as he was, consisted largely in just such a disclosure of unifying ideas, he became something like Emerson's ideal scientist, one 'always watching for the glimmering of that pure, plastic Idea.'

Accordingly, Emerson was on the whole unsympathetic with the patient experimentation on which scientific achievement is based and prescribed instead a moral and spiritual reformation in the scientist. Scientists will never understand nature, he wrote in *Nature,* using Swedenborgian language, until they approach her in the fire of holiest affections, and not simply with the intellect. It was the duty of the naturalist, he wrote in an early lecture, to study in faith and in love; or, as he put it in 1840, 'science always goes abreast with the just elevation of the man. . . .'

With this view of science, it would appear that there was small hope of culture, in Emerson's sense, in the study of science, since the elevation culture was intended to bring about was necessary to make true science possible. And in point of fact he did not look to science much to coax and woo the great instinct; rather 'the greatest office of natural science [is] . . . to explain man to himself,' to help him to understand if not to heal his divided nature. The scientist, like the true orator, should be one 'who could reconcile your moral character and your natural history, who could explain your misfortunes, your fevers, your debts, your temperament, your habits of thought, your tastes, and in every explanation not sever you from the Whole, but unite you to it. . . .' In the rare moments of union with the Whole such questionings dropped away. Generally, however, as he put it, 'I have this latent omniscience coexistent with omnignorance.' Knowledge of the One did not explain the Many; The Idea according to which the Universe is made is wholly wanting to us. . . .' For this reason, we may suppose, the idea of evolution, throwing nature into the perspective of a new unifying idea, was able to catch his imagination in his later life. He accepted it uncritically as a conspicuous confirmation of his hope that science might 'uncover the living ligaments . . . which attach the dull men and things we converse with, to the splendor of the First Cause. . . .'

The Idea of nature Emerson desired, needless to say, was not forthcoming; the inspiration he sought from nature's influence was evanescent and illusory. Man could not immerse himself in the unconsciousness of nature, nor could he conquer her through consciousness, by achieving her explanation. He imaged his frustration in a series of mythological parallels. Nature was the Sphinx, asking her riddle of each passerby. She was Proteus, whose meanings changed as often as she was studied. Her lover was Tantalus, baffled by an apparent wealth of meaning that withdrew as often as he tried to seize it. Nature was an enchanted circle, which he was forbidden to enter. Like some creature of old romance, the 'universal dame' repeated her old challenge:

> Who telleth one of my meanings
> Is master of all I am.

But he knew that a hero with stronger magic than a mere sauntering poet could command would be needed to lift her spell. Nature served as a perpetual mute invitation to man to assume his rightful lordship but had no power to teach him to accept it. As he summed it up in a lecture, 'The co-presence of the living Soul is essential to all teaching.'

But this same fatal flaw held true of *all* the means of culture. In his lecture on 'The School,' for example, he spoke of persons and books as two of man's teachers. But these, which may be taken to sum up between them the cultural influences of man, as opposed to nature, had the same unpredictability. Emerson read books for scarcely any other reason than to provide himself with a stimulus to inspiration, 'for the lustres,' as he said, and

was often successful. Yet books were, after all, but black marks
on paper. They could live only with the life of the reader. 'As
the proverb says, "He that would bring home the wealth of the
Indies, must carry out the wealth of the Indies." . . . When
the mind is braced by labor and invention, the page of whatever
book we read becomes luminous with manifold allusion.' Again,
the soul illumines the book, not the book the soul.

Persons, the conversation of contemporaries, were a still more
uncertain means. Emerson summed up the situation when he
wrote in 'Friendship,' 'I do then with my friends as I do with
my books.' Exactly—and as was true of books, a response to
friends required 'the uprise of nature in us to the same degree
it is in them.' All came back in the end to instinct, the primary
teacher. 'Persons I labor at, and grope after, and experiment
upon, make continual effort at sympathy, which sometimes is
found and sometimes is missed; but I tire at last, and the fruit
they bring to my intellect or affections is oft small and poor.
But a thought has its own proper motion which it communicates
to me, not borrows of me, and on its Pegasus back I override
and overlook the world.'

The whole matter of the means of culture is summed up in
one sentence in his journals: 'A day is a rich abyss of means,
yet mute and void.' The poem Emerson wrote thirteen years
later on this theme, 'Days,' testifies to his lasting regret at not
achieving his morning wishes, but in its implied self-reproach
is not representative of his by then settled acquiescence in the
irremediable waywardness of the divine uprush of soul through
which alone they could become reality.

Yet we would mistake his mood if we supposed that he ever
finally despaired of culture. A day *was* a rich abyss of means.
The daily anticipation, often rewarded, that the whole solid
world might roll aside like a mist and show the living soul
underneath, was ground for an ever-renewed hope, not despair.
If we find that the days pass by and we are still the same, yet
we can believe that the years teach much which the days never
knew. As a ship advances by a succession of tacks, 'so in life our
profession, our amusements, our errors even, give us with much

parade, or with our own blushes, a little solid wisdom.' The upper world is always there, like the air we breathe, even when we are not aroused to awareness of it. How can it fail to affect us? 'Every moment instructs, and every object; for wisdom is infused into every form. It has been poured into us as blood; it convulsed us as pain; it slid into us as pleasure; it enveloped us in dull, melancholy days, or in days of cheerful labor; we did not guess its essence until after a long time.'

Significant effect over time

CHAPTER FIVE

Circles

ABOUT 1840, Emerson entered a period of comparative unsettlement in his thoughts from which proceed some of his most interesting essays. Numerous indications, in them and in his journals, betray his disturbed awareness that the pattern of his first convictions is undergoing an unforeseen modification, and that the various truths he has come to recognize are in radical and permanent conflict with each other. This new mood marks, for example, the most unsettled and unsettling of his *Essays, First Series,* the essay 'Circles.' Largely written new for this volume, it stands on the edge between the earlier and later periods in his thought and shows internal evidence that his thought is in a state of transition.

Its main theme, that 'Intellect is progress forevermore,' is by no means a new thought to him. As his son Edward Emerson suggests, the essay should be read in connection with 'Uriel,' for it also, like the poem, celebrates the subversive power of a new idea. Both say, in effect, 'Beware when the great God lets loose a thinker on this planet.' Both speak for Emerson's pride in the explosive properties of his thought, and his ill-concealed delight at the thought of the havoc he could wreak—if people were once to listen to him. It thus emphatically belongs among his revolutionary utterances. 'I unsettle all things,' he says, by way of warning; but no one can miss the ring of pride.

Yet intermingled with this celebration of the power of thought to destroy the routine of society is another note of a less assured kind—a fresh consciousness of impermanence in his own thought. His own convictions too are unsettled. The familiar principle that no belief or institution is final, which he accepted easily as long as he felt himself the innovator, has acquired a new import for him, now that he finds some of his own beliefs losing substance. 'Our life is an apprenticeship,' he begins, 'to the truth that around every circle another can be drawn; . . . that there is always another dawn risen on mid-noon, and under every deep a lower deep opens'—a confession whose full force we catch when we recall the use of the same reminiscence of Milton earlier in the journals: '. . . the common life is an endless succession of phantasms; and long after we have deemed ourselves recovered and sound, light breaks in upon us and we find we have yet had no sane hour. Another morn rises on mid-noon'; and notice also the possible allusion to a line by his young friend, W. E. Channing, that was to become a favorite with him:

> If my bark sinks, 'tis to another sea.[1]

A little later we find the exhortation, clearly applicable to his own case: 'Fear not the new generalization. Does the fact look crass and material, threatening to degrade thy theory of spirit? Resist it not; it goes to refine and raise thy theory of matter just as much.' This recalls a similar adjuration in his journals of the same period: 'The method of advance in nature is perpetual transformation. Be ready to emerge from the chrysalis of today, its thoughts and institutions, as thou hast come out of the chrysalis of yesterday.

'Every new thought which makes day in our souls has its long morning twilight to announce its coming.'

The upshot is a renewed stress on the active soul. The thought in the strength of which he took up his revolutionary position— that positive power was all—is now in turn shaken by the growing realization that negative power, or circumstance, is half. As a consequence he feels momentarily thrown back on the perception of the moment. 'No facts are to me sacred; none are profane; I simply experiment, an endless seeker with no Past at

---

[1] A more hopeful expression in its context than it seems by itself:
> I am not earth-born, though I here delay;
> Hope's child, I summon infiniter powers,
> And laugh to see the mild and sunny day
> Smile on the shrunk and thin autumnal hours.
> I laugh, for Hope hath happy place with me:
> If my bark sinks, 'tis to another sea.

my back.' In a similar spirit he wrote that part of the essay 'Self-Reliance' which he afterwards said would have been better written, 'Damn consistency!' What matters is not any thought, but the thinking. In the immortal energy of mind lies the compensation for the mortality of truth. 'Valor consists in the power of self-recovery, so that a man cannot have his flank turned, cannot be out-generalled, but put him where you will, he stands. This can only be by his preferring truth to his past apprehension of truth, and his alert acceptance of it from whatever quarter; the intrepid conviction that his laws, his relations to society, his Christianity, his world, may at any time be superseded and decease.'

'Life only avails, not the having lived. . . . Neither thought nor virtue will keep, but must be refreshed by new today.' This more personal and urgent application of Emerson's old recommendation to live in the present accounts for the unusually restless mood of this essay. He comes for the moment to echo a strain of Romantic thought not generally characteristic of him, the ideal of striving as an end in itself, the Browningesque moral ideal of a *Strebung nach Unendliche*. Life was a pursuit 'of the Unattainable, the flying Perfect, around which the hands of man can never meet, at once the inspirer and the condemner of every success.' It demanded a 'continual effort to raise himself above himself, to work a pitch above his last height. . . .' At whatever human cost, one must keep growing, or die on the vine.

The restlessness of this essay infects even his conception of the Soul itself. The incessant creative energy of the World-Soul, conspicuous in his later evolutionary thinking, appropriately governs this essay. 'Whilst the eternal generation of circles proceeds, the eternal generator abides. . . . Forever it labors to create a life and thought as large and excellent as itself, but in vain, for that which is made instructs how to make a better.' Its incessant creative labor sets man a strenuous example. To live in the soul, to follow nature, is to be continuously creative, and never to pause or rest. 'In nature every moment is new; the past is always swallowed and forgotten; the coming only is sacred. Nothing is secure but life, transition, the energizing spirit. . . . People wish to be settled; only as far as they are unsettled is there any hope for them.'

This essay shows signs that Emerson at the time of writing was appreciably unsettled; but that there is any hope for him, in the sense in which he means it here, is more doubtful. The eternal generator is always alive and changes only in his works. But the radical defect of man, the creator in the finite, is his incapacity to maintain his creative force. 'The only sin is limitation'—but this is original sin beyond the power of grace. A limitary instinct opposes the expansive one, and the counteraction of the two forms the chequered pattern of human life. Here Emerson stresses the expansive force, the ground of hope. But the weight of his experience as a whole told on the other side. Every man believes that he has a greater possibility—but every man learns that it is beyond his reach. 'Alas for this infirm faith, this will not strenuous, this vast ebb of a vast flow! I am God in nature; I am a weed by the wall.'

Here is Emerson's deepest disillusionment, deeper than his disaffection with the ideal of great action, though bound up with it: the infirmity of faith. The experience of the Deity in the soul, that seems when present to 'confer a sort of omnipresence and omnipotence which asks nothing of duration, but sees that the energy of the mind is commensurate with the work to be done, without time,' is inherently and necessarily transient and confers in the long run nothing but a tantalizing promise and a glorious memory. It lifts one above circumstances, beyond all limits, out of time; yet it is itself subject to time, limits, and circumstance and obeys its own insurmountable laws of ebb and flow. Time and experience are teaching Emerson to respect their dominion. His transcendentalism is steadily giving way to a basic empiricism—one which, though it includes and stresses man's peculiar experience of the Soul, nevertheless pragmatically recognizes the priority of experience over 'Reality.'

At the heart of this later empiricism is a new respect for time. Originally, part of the revolution to which he had looked forward was a release from subjection to time. As he wrote in 1838:

'A great man escapes out of the kingdom of time; he puts time under his feet.' His revolt against tradition had been designed to cut the traces that bound him to history and bring him to live, not in the kingdom of time, but in direct contact with the divine life beyond and above time. 'Man . . . cannot be happy and strong until he . . . lives with nature in the present, above time.'

'A moment is a concentrated eternity,' he wrote in 1836. The phrase points up the paradox implicit in his ambition to live in a present above time. He did not wish to be rapt into eternity, but to live in an Eternal Now. He at first thought of his Eternal Now as a permanent condition of poise and self-sufficiency, like the motionless center of a moving wheel. But actually, since his eternity was a moment, at every moment eternity slipped away from him. His ambition to live in the present, above time, meant that every present moment was a new crisis, without support from the one just past nor help for the one to come. Eventually, Emerson was brought to admit the fallacy of his notion of an Eternal Now, and to concede that all his life, ecstasies as well as prosaic details, was and must be subject to the passage of time. From the 1840's onward dates his intense consciousness of the unceasing onward flow of time, a flowing that comes to signify to him, not the perpetual creative revolution celebrated in 'Circles,' but rather the stream of everything that runs away. He was often understandably distressed by this incessant flux. 'If the world would only wait one moment, if a day could now and then be intercalated, which should be no time, but pause and landing-place, a vacation during which sun and star, old age and decay, debts and interest of money, claims and duties, should all intermit and be suspended for the halcyon trance. . . . But this on, on, forever onward, wears out adamant.' The evanescence and lubricity of all objects is lamented in 'Experience' as the most unhandsome part of our condition.

Yet 'even in the midst of his moods of regret,' F. O. Matthiessen has pointed out, 'that the days were slipping past without fulfillment, he did not doubt that his course was right. Out of the depth of his consent to his lot welled up the opposite

mood, his dilation in response to the flux.' Perhaps the best
expression of this consent to the universal flowing is his poem
'Two Rivers.' The finished poem is only a dilution of the first
impromptu prose 'thought':

'Thy voice is sweet, Musketaquid, and repeats the music of
the rain, but sweeter is the silent stream which flows even
through thee, as thou through the land.

'Thou art shut in thy banks, but the stream I love flows in
thy water, and flows through rocks and through the air and
through rays of light as well, and through darkness, and
through men and women.

'I hear and see the inundation and the eternal spending of the
stream in winter and in summer, in men and animals, in
passion and thought. Happy are they who can hear it.'

An admission that his spiritual life was subject to time may
seem a small concession, particularly as in a part of his mind he
had always known that it was so. 'As the law of light is, fits of
easy transmission and reflexion, such is also the soul's law,' he
had written in 1833, and quoted Wordsworth:

> 'T is the most difficult of tasks to keep
> Heights which the soul is competent to gain.

Forty years later, in his essay 'Inspiration,' he was still quoting
the same lines from Wordsworth and conceded, as the sun of
a lifetime's wisdom, that 'what we want is consecutiveness. 'T is
with us a flash of light, then a long darkness, then a flash again.'
And in this essay, as at previous times, he explores the means of
cultivating inspiration and suggests some nine disciplines or
circumstances favorable to it. In his search for the *'modus'* of
inspiration faith and scepticism were always mixed and changed
only in their proportions. But that small change made all the
difference.

The extent of that change becomes more apparent when we
notice that, in this late essay, two of the primary conditions he
lays down for inspiration are health and youth. 'We must prize
our own youth. Later, we want heat to execute our plans: the
good will, the knowledge, the whole armory of means are all

present, but a certain heat that once used not to fail, refuses its office, and all is vain until this capricious fuel is supplied.' And again, 'Health is the first muse. . . .' So in 1845 he speaks of genius as before he spoke of heroism: 'Genius consists in health, in plenipotence of that "top of condition" which allows of not only exercise but frolic of faculty.'

He has come almost to concede the natural basis of inspiration. As he notes in this essay, 'It seems a semi-animal heat; as if tea, or wine, or sea-air, or mountains, or a genial companion, or a new thought suggested in book or conversation could fire the train, wake the fancy and the clear perception.' In the 1840's he more and more often ascribes the power of performance, not to an influx of the divine, but to animal spirits; and, whereas he speaks of the first with hope, of the last he uses almost a valetudinarian tone. 'The capital defect of my nature for society . . . is the want of animal spirits. They seem to me a thing incredible, as if God should raise the dead. I hear of what others perform by their aid, with fear.' There is some pathos in Emerson's never wholly daunted quest for the means to stir an instinct which at the same time he knew to depend on a vital force which he could never win. The note is perceptible in such a poem as 'Bacchus.' It is epitomized in a wry entry in his journal for 1842: 'I have so little vital force that I could not stand the dissipation of a flowing and friendly life; I should die of consumption in three months. But now I husband all my strength in this bachelor life I lead; no doubt shall be a well-preserved old gentleman.'

Emerson's recognition of the affinity of the natural vigor of youth and inspiration appears surprisingly early, in one of the most enlightening of his unpublished lectures, the sixth of his course on *Human Life,* called 'The Protest.' Here he expounds, already a little reminiscently, his own protest against the actual. He speaks of it not as his own, but as that of the Youth, and we infer from the lecture that the youth's protest against society is not altogether Emerson's. He is already too old to share the youth's single-minded zeal; he is an 'old stager of society,' the youth 'fantastic' and 'extravagant.' Yet Emerson's tone is not one of superiority, but rather one of envy. 'The heart of Youth is the regenerator of society; the perpetual hope; the incessant effort of recovery. . . . Well for it if it can abide by its Protest. . . . The world has no interest so deep as to cherish that resistance. . . .

'[The young] alone have dominion of the world, for they walk in it with a free step. . . . Each young soul . . . represents the Soul and nothing less.'

The lecture should be read together with 'Circles,' of which it is a forerunner. There also Emerson praises 'Infancy, youth, receptive, aspiring, with religious eye looking upward,' which 'counts itself nothing and abandons itself to the instruction flowing from all sides.' In 'Circles' youth is the condition of creative energy; correspondingly, 'old age seems the only disease. . . . We call it by many names,—fever, intemperance, insanity, stupidity and crime; they are all forms of old age; they are rest, conservatism, appropriation, inertia; not newness, not the way onward. We grizzle every day.'

In the essay, youth and age are not a matter of birthdays, but are spiritual principles that divide life between them. When we live with the soul, we are young; when we fall away from it, we fall again into the power of time. Yet the metaphor is a powerful one, since it recalls the power of time at the moment that it denies it. If the presence of the soul always brings youth, yet youth is the time when the soul best loves to be present. Time is the enemy of faith. In the same manner Emerson contrasted morning and evening, as when he spoke of his morning wishes in 'Days.' 'That is morning, to cease for a bright hour to be a prisoner of this sickly body, and to become as large as nature.'

In 'Circles' Emerson defies time. 'This old age ought not to creep on a human mind,' he asserts. 'I see no need of it. Whilst we converse with what is above us, we do not grow old, but grow young.' And the original journal entry continues, 'Is it possible a man should not grow old? I will not answer for this crazy body. It seems a ship which carries him through the waves of this world and whose timbers contract barnacles and dry-rot, and will not serve for a second course. But I refuse to admit this appeal to the old people we know as valid against a good hope. For do we know one who is an organ of the Holy Ghost?' 'The World-Soul' echoes this denial of age.

> Spring still makes spring in the mind
>   When sixty years are told;
> Love wakes anew this throbbing heart,
>   And we are never old . . .

Courageous words! But in 'The Protest' we find a different and less happy account of the part played in life by 'old age.' The lecture attempts to explain the opposition the youth encounters and in so doing elaborates an Emersonian version of the Fall of Man. For once Emerson blames, not society and the slavish actual, but a failure of force, complementary to inspiration, inherent in every individual.

What is the front the world always shows to the young Spirit? Strange to say, The Fall of Man. . . .
. . . There is somewhat infirm and retreating in every action; a pause of self-praise: a second thought. He has done well and he says, I have done well, and lo! this is the beginning of ill. He is encumbered by his own Past. His past hour mortgages the present hour. Yesterday is the enemy of Today. . . .
This Pause is fatal. Sense pauses: the soul pauses not. In its world is incessant onward movement. Genius has no retrospect. Virtue has no memory. And that is the law for man. Live without interval: if you rest on your oars, if you stop, you fall. He only is wise who thinks now; who reproduces all his experience for the present exigency; as a man stands on his feet only by a perpetual play and adjustment of the muscles. . . .
This old age; this ossification of the heart; this fat in the brain, this degeneracy; is the Fall of Man.

Here Emerson recognizes that the life of the Soul must be without interval, as he does in 'Circles'; but he recognizes, too, the impossibility of such a life for man, subject as he is to an 'old age' that must keep him from ever becoming part or parcel of God. We can see in this lecture that he has begun to notice an effect of time more inexorable than the quick end it brings to any particular moment of inspiration—the long slow ebb of his power to rise to inspiration at all. The process of growing old was a long declension from his birthright. Read autobiographically, the lecture has considerable poignancy.

With this submission to time and fate, all that Emerson called condition came to assume a reality for him that rivaled that of the Soul. From identifying his real self primarily with the divine Self within him and dismissing the rest as outer shell, temporary and apparent, he came to recognize that his real self was his whole contradictory nature, divine potentiality and mortal limits together. 'Then the fact that we lie open to God, and what may he not do!

'But no, we can predict very well that, though new thoughts may come, and cheer, and gild, they shall not transport us. There are limits to our mutability. Time seems to make these shadows that we are, tough and peakèd.' As F. I. Carpenter has wisely remarked, 'He changed his allegiance from the world of pure thought to that of experience.' This change marks the end of any real belief on Emerson's part in the rationality of life. Always baffled by the problem of the Individual, he now found himself so inextricably involved in contradictions that he made inconsistency the test of true speech. 'We must reconcile the contradictions as we can, but their discord and their concord introduce wild absurdities into our thinking and speech. No sentence will hold the whole truth, and the only way in which we can be just, is by giving ourselves the lie. . . . All the universe over, there is but one thing, this old Two-Face, creator-creature, mind-matter, right-wrong, of which any proposition may be affirmed or denied.' Once he had accepted the defeat of his first hopes, he regularly took for granted the inherent absurdity of the human situation.

But the defeat of his early dreams of victory must not be overstated. The promise of the Soul remained, though all experience told against it. With the loss of his immediate expectations he appealed to the indefinite future; he retreated in good

order to a prepared position. The individual seeks for the means
to rise to a heroic life—in vain; he abstains from routine, ceases
to put up bars and impediments, and waits for the rightful flood
of Power. Nothing happens. What then? 'Our philosophy is to
wait. We have retreated on Patience, transferring our oft-
shattered hope now to larger and eternal good.' 'Patience,—
patience,' was the counsel even of the American scholar. The
transcendentalist had learned the same lesson: 'Patience, and
still patience.' This was still the last word in Emerson's report
on 'Experience': 'Patience and patience, we shall win at the
last.' He had to concede, 'We have no one example of the
poetic life realized, therefore all we say seems bloated.' Yet 'to
my soul the day does not seem dark, nor the cause lost. . . .
Patience and truth, patience with our own frost and negations,
and few words must serve. . . . If our sleeps are long, if our
flights are short, if we are not plumed and painted like orioles
and Birds of Paradise, but like sparrows and plebean birds, if
our taste and training are earthen, let that fact be humbly and
happily borne with. . . . Perhaps all that is not performance is
preparation, or performance that shall be.'
   And beneath this consent to his long sleep we can still hear
mutterings of the old defiance. Emerson's faith in the greatness
of man was not destroyed, but driven underground. If he came
to concede the inescapable power of the actual, to believe in fate,
he never accommodated his claims to this acknowledged fact.
He recognized his empirical limitations but, like a deposed
monarch, gave up none of his pretensions to sovereignty, for all
that he could perceive no way to attain his throne. '. . . there
ought to be no such thing as Fate,' he wrote one year after the
above passage. 'As long as we use this word, it is a sign of our
impotence and that we are not yet ourselves. . . . whilst this Deity
glows at the heart, and by his unlimited presentiments gives me
all Power, I know that to-morrow will be as this day, I am a
dwarf, and I remain a dwarf. That is to say, I believe in Fate.
As long as I am weak, I shall talk of Fate; whenever the God
fills me with his fulness, I shall see the disappearance of Fate.'
   One ground at least of his never-waning interest in great

men was his hope to see achieved in him 'that shall come' the success to the senses which his lack of vital force forbade in him. And the basis of this hope of a vicarious success to the senses is the fact that, to the soul, he is a victor now. No concessions to the actual can affect or dim the Deity that glows at the heart and gives him all power. Emerson was thinking of that 'Religious Intellect,' Charles King Newcomb, but also speaking for himself, when he quoted 'Benedict' in 'Worship': 'I am never beaten until I know that I am beaten. . . . in all the encounters that have yet chanced, I have not been weaponed for that particular occasion, and have been historically beaten; and yet I know all the time that I have never been beaten; have never yet fought, shall certainly fight when my hour comes, and shall beat.'

'I am *Defeated* all the time; yet to Victory I am born.'

PART II

F A T E

CHAPTER SIX

Skepticism

ALTHOUGH Emerson refused to conceive of life as tragedy, there is a sense in which his view of life can properly be called tragic, in so far as his recognition of the limits of mortal condition meant a defeat of his first romance of self-union and greatness. To be forced to recognize that men are not gods may not seem a tragic destiny, and he learned to accept it cheerfully enough; but in view of man's possibilities, his exclusion from his birthright of freedom and lordship was a genuinely tragic discovery. 'I wish to break all prisons,' he had said, and for a while imagined he might be about to do so. Now he could see that, for all the unceasing affirmation at the bottom of the heart, man would remain, as he had always been, confined to the mill-round of his fate.

This peculiarly Emersonian tragic sense, the elegiac recognition that our life perpetually promises us a glory we will never realize, emerges most clearly in some of his poems. In 'Days,' for example, he betrays a lingering sense of obscure guilt at the contrast between his morning wishes and the few herbs and apples that must be his lot. 'Uriel' allegorizes his lapse as a prophet of truth. The Emersonian despair emerges in 'The World-Soul':

> Alas! the Sprite that haunts us
>   Deceives our rash desire;
> It whispers of the glorious gods,
>   And leaves us in the mire.

It is the subject of 'Bacchus':

> Pour, Bacchus! the remembering wine;
> Retrieve the loss of me and mine!
>   .   .   .   .
> Haste to cure the old despair,—

109

> Reason in Nature's lotus drenched,
> The memory of ages quenched;
>
> .   .   .   .
> Let wine repair what this undid . . .

It is the subject, again, of 'Ode to Beauty'; we catch it inciden-
tally in 'Friendship'; it is the basis of the expostulation with the
gods of 'Alphonso of Castile.'

It appears most interestingly in a poem apparently prompted
by the 1837 depression, 'The Humble-Bee':

> .   .   .   .
> Wiser far than human seer,
> Yellow-breeched philosopher!
> Seeing only what is fair,
> Sipping only what is sweet,
> Thou dost mock at fate and care,
> Leave the chaff, and take the wheat.
> When the fierce northwestern blast
> Cools sea and land so far and fast,
> Thou already slumberest deep;
> Woe and want thou canst outsleep;
> Want and woe, which torture us,
> Thy sleep makes ridiculous.

For all the idyllic celebration of nature and summer in this
poem, it is basically tragic. One recalls, for contrast, the conclusion of *Nature:* 'As when the summer comes from the south
the snow-banks melt and the face of the earth becomes green
before it, so shall the advancing spirit create its ornaments along
its path, and carry with it the beauty it visits and the song which
enchants it; it shall draw beautiful faces, warm hearts, wise discourse, and heroic acts, around its way, until evil is no more seen.'
Now, not without an irony that recalls Swift's Houyhnhnms,
Emerson celebrates the eternal summer of the humble-bee—how
different from man's inevitable winter! The balance of the sea-
sons in this poem exactly expresses the special blend of faith
and scepticism which came habitually to mark his later attitude
toward life. At the same time, there is no notion of learning by
suffering here. The wise man knows that, to the Soul, want and

woe are temporary and unreal; nevertheless, they will always
continue to torture us.

Man is promised the world—a promise perpetually renewed
and never kept. Comparing the claims of faith with the ob-
served facts, Emerson finds certain radical discrepancies. As a
result, something recalling the scepticism that prompted his
early doubts of 'Rational Christianity' rises to question their
solution in transcendentalism.[1] His acceptance of limitations
precipitates a basic adjustment of belief.

The chief testament of this newly empirical Emerson is the
essay 'Experience.' Here he 'set his heart on honesty' and wrote
down as accurately as he could a description of man's condition.
Yet there is, we must remember, a reservation implicit even in
his title. The Soul, he had always insisted, contradicts all experience. Hence there is a certain implication in the title that this
is a lower subject, like 'Prudence,' or 'Domestic Life,' and several times during the essay Emerson stops to point out that the
limitations of experience that he is describing do not affect his
faith in the Soul, which, resting as it does on a direct intuition,
is its own evidence, not to be shaken by any contrary experience.

The essay might have been called 'An Interim Report on an
Experiment in Self-Reliance.' 'I am not the novice I was fourteen, nor yet seven years ago,' he wrote at its conclusion; and its
tone is no longer the confident exhortation of 'Self-Reliance.'
Now he finds that the self on which he would rely is governed
by an incongruous set of conditions which he can neither reconcile nor control. Of the seven lords of life which the essay considers, four are conditions which operate to thwart the power of
the divine within the soul. That Reality should ever break
through such barriers and surprise the soul at all is the standing
miracle of mortal life, and like all miracles is unpredictable,
inexplicable, and rare.

As the whole course of this study should help to show, and

[1] See Chapter 1.

as his journals confirm, the subject matter of this essay has an importance for Emerson second only to the intuitions of his faith. It is by no means a more or less formal attempt to do justice to the other side of the question of belief, as if the points he raised were merely speculative ones that did not touch him personally, 'Sunday objections, made up on purpose to be put down.' In the growing drift and flow of all things, Emerson is trying to place himself, to reach at least that measure of control over his fate that will enable him to understand where he is going and what is happening to him. He knows that he has always an answer to the problems he raises, that the Soul is a standing refuge. 'If my bark sink, 't is to another sea.' But why should it sink? Why attempt to put to sea at all in a vessel that must be 'rent to chips and splinters in this storm of many elements?' 'We want a ship in these billows we inhabit . . . tight, and fit to the form of man. . . .' Study what man is, then, not what he should be, and follow these specifications; assemble a philosophy of experience.

Evidence is not lacking in other essays, as in his letters and journals, that Emerson, for all his trust in the Soul, was steadily collecting materials for such a philosophy. His continued concern with the problem prompted a second attempt to formulate and come to terms with it in his chapter on Montaigne in *Representative Men.*

The intention of this essay is not altogether the same as that of 'Experience.' It is not ostensibly a report on his personal experience, but a statement of the philosophy of a newcomer to his intellectual drama, the Skeptic.[2] The name is an even more forceful reminder that Emerson had reservations about the philosophy of experience which he ascribed to the skeptic, for the skeptic is of course the traditional enemy of faith. Skepticism was a half-truth; it ignored the facts on which faith was founded. The skeptic was a lineal descendant of the conservative,[3] and like him was partial and false.

At the same time the conservative and the skeptic were im-

2 On Emerson's two spellings of this term, see p. 9.
3 See pp. 80-81.

pregnable on their own premises. Just as Emerson had personified his revolutionary ambitions in the hero-type of the scholar, so now he put his doubts of the scholar's faith into the mouth of the skeptic. By thus creating a fictitious *alter ego* to whom to attribute his more dangerous thoughts, Emerson could relieve himself of responsibility for them and yet at the same time give them expression. The doubts of the skeptic remain his own, however, though detached; his skepticism is his most considered summary of his antitranscendentalism. The name he gave it shows his continued faith; yet his concern with it equally reveals the adjustment to fact that his faith was undergoing.

To a certain extent, Emerson felt that his faith *was* skepticism. Like his 'students,' his deeper belief began in unbelief. This sense of the term flickers in and out of the essay on Montaigne and contributes not a little to the ambiguous impression of that essay. There now and again he appears to use the name skeptic for the rebel against tradition which he himself started out to be. 'Great believers are always reckoned infidels, impracticable, fantastic, atheistic, and really men of no account. The spiritualist finds himself driven to express his faith by a series of skepticisms.' The skepticism in these passages is the skepticism of Uriel.

Between the extremes of the 'Hume' and the 'Uriel' senses of skepticism falls the conception of the 1840's. The skeptic is midway between the 'materialist' and the 'abstractionist.' In rejecting these extremes, Emerson's most vigorous condemnation is reserved, as we might expect, for the 'scoffer,' the unmitigated materialist. More interesting, however, is his rejection of the materialist's opposite number, the abstractionist. Emerson here takes a common-sense view of the transcendentalist, the reformer, and men of faith generally. Though this foreshortened point of view is the skeptic's, not Emerson's, it offers an instructive foil to the vast claims of *The American Scholar*.

The leading characteristic of the abstractionists is their arrogance. 'It is not strange that these men, remembering what they have seen and hoped of ideas, should affirm disdainfully the superiority of ideas. Having at some time seen that the happy soul will carry all the arts in power, they say, Why cumber ourselves with superfluous realizations? and like dreaming beggars they assume to speak and act as if these values were already substantiated.' Yet how febrile all this is! 'The studious class are their own victims; they are thin and pale, their feet are cold, their heads are hot, the night is without sleep, the day a fear of interruption,—pallor, squalor, hunger and egotism. If you come near them and see what conceits they entertain,—they are abstractionists, and spend their days and nights in dreaming some dream; in expecting the homage of society to some precious scheme, built on a truth, but destitute of proportion in its presentment, of justness in its application, and of all energy of will in the schemer to embody and vitalize it.'

It is not hard to catch the reference to such as Alcott here, and yet this is clearly also a self-caricature. The comparison of the abstractionists to 'dreaming beggars' recalls an inverse passage in 'Self-Reliance': '. . . man . . . is in the world a sort of sot, but now and then wakes up, exercises his reason and finds himself a true prince.' The power of thought, of the ideal over the actual— what else had he himself been proclaiming all this time? But to Emerson in his skeptical moods, thought becomes just—thought. 'Come, no chimeras! . . . Let us have a robust, manly life. . . . Let us have to do with real men and women, and not with skipping ghosts.'

Man cannot live by ideas alone. Skepticism is a more than half-serious experiment in a metaphysics of empiricism prompted by the bankruptcy of transcendentalism. Caught between the everlasting Yea and the everlasting No, Emerson will try how it feels at the 'centre of indifference.' When the debate is closed, and the roll called, Emerson continues to cast his vote with the believers. But the failure of his initial transcendentalism to allow for all his experience impels him to work out for himself, as a counterbalancing hypothesis, what life would look like if experience and not faith should be given the last word.

Above all, a realistic empiricism would avoid *a priori* claims. Skepticism recognized the inadequacy of theories; for every statement there was a counterstatement, to each mood succeeded another mood. More deeply, skepticism rested on the perception that faith alone did not solve the question of the conduct or the explanation of life. 'Why pretend that life is so simple a game, when we know how subtle and elusive the Proteus is?' Skepticism would lay the emphasis on fidelity to fact. 'The philosophy we want is one of fluxions and mobility. . . . The soul of man must be the type of our scheme, just as the body of man is the type after which a dwelling-house is built.'

The skeptic's view of the soul of man is ridiculously far from the grand egoism of the transcendentalist. '. . . we cannot give ourselves too many advantages in this unequal conflict, with powers so vast and unweariable ranged on one side, and this little conceited vulnerable popinjay that a man is, bobbing up and down into every danger, on the other.' For the potential God, 'open on one side to the deeps of spiritual nature,' he substitutes a neutral personality open, as it were, on all sides, adrift on the stream of time and circumstance, and oriented only by certain landmarks which in 'Experience' Emerson called the lords of life. These he could not explain, but only observe and reconcile as he might. To call the roll of these guardians was as close as the skeptic could come to a philosophy of life.

Both 'Experience' and 'Montaigne' agree on the chief ground of skepticism; it is 'the doctrine of the Illusionists,' The condition of man is to be cut off from the real. '. . . souls never touch their objects. An innavigable sea washes with silent waves between us and the things we aim at and converse with.' 'Dream delivers us to dream, and there is no end to illusion.' Emerson's Oriental reading, which did not shape his transcendentalism, now helps him to express his dismay at the 'stunning non-intercourse law' that cuts men off from the world, from other men, and from the underlying Reality. '. . . we may come to accept it as the fixed rule and theory of our state of education, that God is a substance, and his method is illusion. The Eastern sages owned the goddess Yoganidra, the great illusory energy of Vishnu, by whom, as utter ignorance, the whole world is beguiled.'

But it was not the unreality of the object that most disturbed Emerson; it was the unreality of the subject. Man himself was an illusion. 'Ghost-like we glide through nature, and should not know our place again.' Not the dreams, but the dreaming, is the crucial check to the affirmative impulse. 'There are moods in which we court suffering, in the hope that here at least we shall find reality, sharp peaks and edges of truth. . . . [But] That, like all the rest, plays about the surface, and never introduces me into the reality. . . . Nothing is left us now but death. We look to that with a grim satisfaction, saying, There at least is reality that will not dodge us.'

Need we pay Emerson the doubtful compliment of insisting that he did not really mean these things, that he did not in fact know moods in which the thought of suffering and even of death gave him a grim satisfaction, as preferable to his present fate? Perhaps it is more of a compliment to his humanity to insist that he did. The reason why he did is not obscure. The breach through which a sense of illusion was able at times to flood his life was the old fact of his powerlessness. He fell prey to it through his surrender to fate. The real sting of the doctrine of the Illusionists is the thought that 'free agency is the emptiest name.' We do not control our fortunes; we cannot even act to modify our character. What growth we do experience is not our doing; perhaps all experiences leave us exactly where they found us. 'We are carried by destiny along our life's course, looking as grave and knowing as little as the infant who is carried in his wicker coach through the street.'

All the grounds for doubt of the skeptic are forms of this sense of subjection to necessity. There is 'Succession swift,' the subjection of man to the flowing of time. Emerson can even call this the secret of the illusoriness, for it means not merely the necessity of a succession of objects, but of moods. 'Life is a train of moods like a string of beads, and as we pass through them they prove to be many-colored lenses which paint the world their own hue, and each shows only what lies in its focus.' When in the mood of faith we believe; when in a skeptical mood we doubt; time, nature, digestion perhaps, control our spiritual life, and not we ourselves. In this mood, this sincerest of men could write, 'I am always insincere, as always knowing there are other moods.'

Then there is the power of temperament—'the iron wire on which the beads are strung.' This also 'enters fully into the system of illusions and shuts us in a prison of glass which we cannot see.' All our experience of impulse and spontaneity is a deception; we will never pass the boundaries of our nature. 'Men resist the conclusion in the morning, but adopt it as the evening wears on, that temper prevails over everything of time, place and condition, and is inconsumable in the flames of religion.'

This last ground of illusion had a particular application to Emerson's own condition, by virtue of his own temperamental necessity to be a scholar, a poet, a man of thought and not of action. One can look on the whole transcendental romance we have watched him spin as a heroic effort to reconcile himself to this fact. A thought can shake the world, he had told himself; the thinker is the greatest actor, the only true master and leader of men; his solitude is not a failure or defect, but a mark of his special destiny; his private thoughts are a means of divine revelation to men. More, every man, even the scholar, has in him the seeds of a greatness that will transcend all limitations; thought is an earnest of performance. But the skeptic disbelieved all this; this was the typical arrogance of the abstractionist. Through the skeptic Emerson turns against himself.

The thinker is self-severed from the robust and manly life of normal society; yet he is severed also from Reality. 'Intellect puts an interval'—an interval even between man and the Soul.' So another ground of doubt for the skeptic is 'the levity of intellect.' The intellect is beholding, not worship, not the uprush of soul that marks a moment of faith.[4] But if thought as well as action is unfriendly to faith, what justifies the practical abstention of the scholar? Let him not aggravate his narrow fate by arrogant pretensions.

[4] Compare pp. 134-35.

The scholar's ethics, the ascetic quest of greatness, had been based on Emerson's faith in man's unlimited possibilities. So the skeptic's opposite recognition of fate and illusion prompted a skeptical ethics. It is a counterstatement to the pretensions of the reformer. The reformer's aim was to liberate the infinite worthiness in man. But this, in Emerson's image, was as much as to attempt to separate the flesh from the spirit, and led only to bewilderment and absurdity. 'There are objections to every course of life and action, and the practical wisdom infers an indifferency. . . . Life is not intellectual or critical, but sturdy. Its chief good is for well-mixed people who can enjoy what they find, without question.'

The ethics of the skeptic are based on life, not as it ought to be, but as it is. His first injunction is, 'Do not craze yourself with thinking, but go about your business anywhere.' He recognizes the permanent limitations of human nature. 'Human life is made up of the two elements, power and form, and the proportion must be invariably kept if we would have it sweet and sound. Each of these elements in excess makes a mischief as hurtful as its defect. . . . A man is a golden impossibility. The line he must walk is a hair's breadth. The wise through excess of wisdom is made a fool.' He substitutes an ethics of balance, an Aristotelian quest of the mean, for the suicidal greatness-or-nothing ethics of transcendentalism. 'I know that human strength is not in extremes, but in avoiding extremes. . . . What is the use of pretending to powers we have not? . . . Why exaggerate the power of virtue? Why be an angel before your time? These strings, wound up too high, will snap. . . . I will try to keep the balance true.' In a world governed so largely by illusion, why try to live by a superhuman reality? 'We live amid surfaces, and the true art of life is to skate well on them.'

So also he sets aside the impossible effort to live above time. The skeptic also would live in the present, but he would do so by foregoing the fanciful hope of an Eternal Now. 'Since our office is with moments, let us husband them. Five minutes of to-day are worth as much to me as five minutes in the next millennium. . . . Men live in their fancy, like drunkards whose hands are too soft and tremulous for successful labor. It is a tempest of fancies, and the only ballast I know is a respect to the present hour.' The only reality that men can achieve lies in honestly living out each moment as it comes. 'To finish the moment, to find the journey's end in every step of the road, to live the greatest number of good hours' is the wisdom of the skeptic. 'To fill the hour,—that is happiness; to fill the hour and leave no crevice for a repentance or an approval.'

The skeptic sees clearly the distinction, denied in the Divinity School *Address*, between natural freedom and moral perfection and unhesitatingly chooses freedom. Our duty is fulfilled if we do broad justice where we are. To postpone and refer and wish in the hope of a supernal perfection is to lose freedom altogether. 'Nature, as we know her, is no saint. . . . Her darlings, the great, the strong, the beautiful, are not children of our law; do not come out of the Sunday School, nor weigh their food, nor punctually keep the commandments.' In the same spirit he accepts his individual genius. Thought, literature, is no grand thing, but it was what he was born to do. Let him obey his bias and fill the hour. 'Life itself is a bubble and a scepticism, and a sleep within a sleep. Grant it, and as much more as they will,—but thou, God's darling! heed thy private dream . . . know that thy life is a flitting state, a tent for a night, and do thou, sick or well, finish that stint.' This is still self-reliance—but now a naturalistic self-reliance without the transcendentalism, based not on faith but on experience.

Although skepticism, as philosophy and as ethics, played an important part in Emerson's thought, he is careful to emphasize that he himself was never a skeptic. As Marius the Epicurean could pursue his cult of the moment only because the finer spiritual breath of Christianity had not yet touched his pagan world, so skepticism was a possible philosophy only for the natural man, a child of nature like Montaigne (as Emerson thought him), uninhibited by paradoxical notions of an Over-Soul. But Emerson did not share his freedom. Skepticism was a provisional resting place, a momentary relief from the problems of mysticism. When it and its problems returned, the skeptic yielded; the scholar had the best of it in the end. 'I play with the miscellany of facts, and take those superficial views which we call skepticism; but I know that they will presently appear to me in that order which makes skepticism impossible.'

The downright practical wisdom of the skeptic leaves the most crucial fact out of account. The philosophy of experience, based on the past, is vulnerable to Surprise. His neat ethics of balance omits the moral sentiment. But *that* fact is the end of skepticism. 'All moods may be safely tried, and their weight allowed to all objections: the moral sentiment as easily outweighs them all, as any one.' Skepticism thus proves a temporary and unreal escape from the problems of the man of faith. It is the product of Emerson's conflict rather than an answer to it. Skepticism speaks for his deepening respect for experience, his sharpened awareness of the actual frailty and insignificance of man. Yet side by side with it stands his old contempt for experience, the unmitigated egoism that respected nothing but the Soul.

This duality of mood appears even in these skeptical essays themselves. Notice, for example, how the motto for 'Experience' concludes:

> Little man, least of all,
> Among the legs of his guardians tall,
> Walked about with puzzled look:—
> Him by the hand dear Nature took;
> Dearest Nature, strong and kind,
> Whispered, 'Darling, never mind!
> To-morrow they will wear another face,
> *The founder thou! these are thy race!*'

From the strained humility of skepticism he springs back to his idealism. If the old confidence in the Deity within was contradicted by the facts, it became that much more intransigeant—moved, in short, that much closer to a plain solipsism.

The same reversal occurs in the section of 'Experience' in which Emerson discusses what he called subjectiveness. An indication of how closely this section echoes his first convictions may be found in the fact that its structure repeats, in abbreviated form, that of the two chapters 'Idealism' and 'Spirit' in *Nature*. Here he reverts to the original source of his present experience of illusion, the intoxicating glimpse of the 'Berkleian philosophy' which had soon expanded into the doctrine of idealism he expounded in *Nature*. It had seemed a good lever then to detach him from the world, to put nature under his feet and to attach him to the Soul—to transfer his sense of reality from effects to the Cause. Now, cut off even by his own thought from the Deity within, the slave and not the master of fate, he appears to be left, as he had feared he might be, 'in the splendid labyrinth of my perceptions, to wander without end.' Then the Berkeleian doubt becomes another form of skepticism. It is not the key to salvation, but rather the Fall of Man. 'It is very unhappy, but too late to be helped, the discovery we have made that we exist. That discovery is called the Fall of Man. Ever afterwards we suspect our instruments. We have learned that we do not see directly, but mediately, and that we have no means of correcting these colored and distorting lenses which we are, or of computing the amount of their errors. Perhaps these subject-lenses have a creative power; perhaps there are no objects.'

Yet without warning, in the middle of a paragraph, with the facility of habit, the old revolution is accomplished once more. Idealism passes into spiritualism; the Fall of Man becomes his salvation. 'The great and crescive self, rooted in absolute nature, supplants all relative existence and ruins the kingdom of mortal friendship and love.' 'The soul is not twin-born but the only begotten, and though revealing itself as child in time, child in appearance, is of a fatal and universal power, admitting no co-life.' Once more the old ethical corollary follows: '. . . we cannot say too little of our constitutional necessity of seeing things under private aspects, or saturated with our humors. And yet is the God the native of these bleak rocks. That need makes in morals the capital virtue of self-trust. We must hold hard to this poverty, however scandalous, and by more vigorous self-recoveries, after the sallies of action, possess our axis more firmly.'

Emerson reiterates his saving gospel: 'the individual is the world.' The assertion grows only more uncompromising under pressure. There is an undertone of individualism-at-any-cost in this section. 'Nature, art, persons, letters, religions, objects, successively tumble in, and God is but one of [our] ideas. Nature and literature are subjective phenomena; every evil and every good thing is a shadow which we cast.' From being the vestibule of the spiritual life, idealism has become rather a final refuge. We foresee the desperate conclusion of Mark Twain's *Mysterious Stranger: 'Nothing* exists; all is a dream.' Illusion, fate, succession, limitation, Reality—

> To-morrow they will wear another face,
> The founder thou! these are thy race!

The changed atmosphere of this sudden reëmergence of the old arrogance is a striking and most revealing fact. His original assertion of the infinitude of the self is brought up sharply here against his recognition of the limitations of the self, and the result is to make his egoism sound less like a first fact, and more like a last resort. Though he has not denied it and will not do so, it is clearly becoming a less usable belief. He uses it here, as he had always used it, to combat his subjection to fate; but the relief it can bring him now is short. His position is such that a lasting release is no longer to be found in egoistic rebellion, but only in acquiescence.

CHAPTER SEVEN

Acquiescence

SOME minds are incapable of skepticism,' Emerson writes in 'Montaigne.' '. . . They may well give themselves leave to speculate, for they are secure of a return.' Similarly in 'Experience' he insists several times on the power of Power to contradict all experience and reaffirms his undiminished assurance of the ideal. Yet he knows that it is not enough to believe by nature, to contradict the skeptic dogmatically (as he several times appears to do in these essays), and 'lie for the right.' What solution can he find for the skepticism bred by the excessive claims of the faith once hailed as the solution to all his doubts?

The best statement of his answer is to be found in the concluding pages of 'Montaigne.' There he is so explicit as to need little commentary.

. . . the incompetency of power is the universal grief of young and ardent minds. They accuse the divine Providence of a certain parsimony. It has shown the heaven and earth to every child and filled him with a desire for the whole; a desire raging, infinite; a hunger, as of space to be filled with planets; a cry of famine, as of devils for souls. Then for the satisfaction,—to each man is administered a single drop, a bead of dew of vital power, *per day,*—a cup as large as space, and one drop of the water of life in it. . . . In every house, in the heart of each maiden and of each boy, in the soul of the soaring saint, this chasm is found,—between the largest promise of ideal power, and the shabby experience.

The expansive nature of truth comes to our succor, elastic, not to be surrounded. Man helps himself by larger generalizations. . . . Things seem to say one thing, and say the reverse. The appearance is immoral; the result is moral. Things seem to tend downward, to justify despondency, to promote rogues, to defeat the just; and by knaves as by martyrs the just cause is carried forward. . . . the world-spirit is a good swimmer, and storms and waves cannot drown

him. He snaps his fingers at laws. and so, throughout history, heaven
seems to affect low and poor means. Through the years and the
centuries, through evil agents, through toys and atoms, a great and
beneficent tendency irresistibly streams.

Let a man learn to look for the permanent in the mutable and fleet-
ing; let him learn to bear the disappearance of things he was wont
to reverence without losing his reverence; let him learn that he is
here, not to work but to be worked upon, and that, though abyss
open under abyss, and opinion displace opinion, all are at last con-
tained in the Eternal Cause:—

'If my bark sink, 't is to another sea.'

The natural believer saves his faith by transferring it from the
impotent self to the all-disposing fate. Before the parsimony of
the God within, he anchors his faith on the God in the universe.
The folly and superficiality of society, the futility of reform, his
own powerlessness, all can be accepted because they are the
work of a great and beneficent tendency, which accomplishes
the just cause even by evil agents. If hope is deferred and lost,
it can be replaced by trust. If protest is futile, it is also needless.
This transfer of his oft-shattered hope now to larger and
eternal good is the emotional basis of Emerson's later serenity.
Through it he rescued his faith from the dilemma induced by
its earlier egoistic formulation and turned defeat into victory.
He appears to have considered this shift a larger generalization
that united the thesis of his transcendentalism and the antithesis
of his skepticism in a synthesis that reconciled both. Larger it
perhaps is, but it is less clearly a synthesis. It makes his earlier
individualism and self-reliance meaningless; at the same time
it still gives the lie direct to the hard facts of experience, and
this without the supposed supporting evidence of unrealized
human capacities to lend it plausibility. Failing to command the
Power that will set him free, he falls back on a renewed submission to the Law which had always complemented it.[1]

If the keynote of his early thought is revolution, that of his
later thought is acquiescence and optimism. From an intense

[1] See Chapter 2, pp. 33-46.

rebellion against the world in the name of the Soul, he moved to a relative acceptance of things as they are, world and Soul together; from teaching men their power to rise above fate, he turned to teaching them how to make the best of it.

One mark of his acquiescence is a growing contentment with his lot. The hopes on which his protest was based were of a greatness over and above his having; but beneath the agitation induced by that glorious possibility we can see even from the start a basic relish for his situation. His release from his profession, his inheritance, his marriage, his country home, and his success as a lecturer and author all made possible a way of life singularly well adapted to his powers and inclinations. If it allowed him for a while to meditate on a way of life finer yet, that was one more of its recommendations. When in 1834 he wrote 'I will thank God of myself and for that I have. . . . I am born tranquil, not a stern economist of Time, but never a keen sufferer. I will not affect to suffer. Be my life then a long gratitude. I will trust my instincts,' he was unmistakably declaring his acceptance. This basic complacence underlay and qualified with its implicit reservation all his talk of renovation and as that subsided became explicitly his primary attitude.

With its emergence goes a dwindling of his first hostility to society. For some reason, his anxiety visibly lessens in the 1840's, and he comes to terms with the outside world. He comes to see that he can participate in society and still be free, that he does not have to master the huge world just to be himself. Some such reconciliation with society, indeed, was forced on him by the dead end to which the pursuit of the heroic life in action brought him; but we are dealing with deeper adjustments, of which the visible course of his thought is as much symptom as cause. Time, maturity, the long reassurance of his quiet and settled life, the increasing esteem of his fellows, all conspired to weaken his distrust and bring him to see that his antagonist was largely an imaginary one.

Yet Emerson's greater acceptance of society and of the order of things as they are does not represent, as one might expect, the total collapse of his original quest of freedom. In his own

view, on the contrary, it brought him closer to success, since the
hopes it replaced were impossible anyway. His first dreams were
based on the enthusiastic assumption that 'the best is the true.'
His later thought is characteristically an affirmation of a *second
best*. If a perfect freedom was clearly out of reach, man's fate
as he found it still turned out to allow him adequate means to
free himself. The two chief second-best means of freedom that
Emerson found were 'obedience to his genius' and 'the habit of
the observer'—Vocation and Intellect.

⧉

By applying the principle of individual vocation, Emerson
contrived to accept the order of society and still not surrender
his freedom. We can best watch this working out in that revealing lecture, 'The Protest.'[2] Though his subject here is the protest of the youth against society, the lecture does not stop with
his protest, but goes on to describe how he may again be reconciled to the society he defies.

. . . this hostile attitude of young persons toward society . . .
makes them very undesirable companions to their friends: queru-
lous, opinionative, impracticable; and, furthermore, it makes them
unhappy in their own solitude. . . . Yet is it . . . a temporary state.
It endures only whilst society seems a thing worthy of great respect,
whilst it retains an excess of influence and daunts the youth by insisting with all its authority upon his adhesion,—whilst his soul points
another and contrary way. Astonished at this irreconcilable diversity,
he stands for a time suspended, and is only able to resist society with
his sturdy Negative. . . .

On the other hand, if the warlike defence he has attempted is
made good by new impulses from within, if he give place to the soul
and worship it, . . . then he has immortal youth. . . . Then it is
presently revealed to him how he should live and work. Quite
naturally his own path opens before him. His object appears; his
aim becomes simple and losing his dread of society which kept him
dumb and paralytic he begins to work according to his faculty. He

<hr>

2 See pp. 100-103.

has done protesting: Now he begins to affirm: all art affirms: and with every new stroke with greater serenity and joy. . . .

On the whole, then, we think that this crisis in the life of each earnest man, which comes in so forbidding and painful aspect, has nothing in it that need °alarm or confound us. It is the inevitable result of the relation of the soul to the existing corruption of society. It puts to the man the question, Will you fulfil the demands of the soul or will you yield yourself to the conventions of the world? In some form the question comes to each. None can escape the challenge. But why need you sit cowering there, pale and pouting, or why with such a mock tragic air affect such a discontent and superiority?

There is nothing to fear. If you would obey the soul, obey it. Do your own work, and you shall have leave to do it. The bugbear of society is only such until you have accepted your own law. Then all omens are good; all stars auspicious; all men your allies; all parts of life take order and beauty.

'Accept your own law,'—is this the simple answer to the braced-up and stilted rejection of the transcendentalist, the insistence on a highest command which could not be met by any means short of inspiration from the Fountain of Love? We may well be disconcerted at the calm injunction, 'If you would obey the soul, obey it,' after all he had to say, even in this lecture, of the impossibility of doing so. An attempted reliance on the aboriginal Self had not freed him; he was forced to accept his impotency. Then what was the secret of a free life? To this question Emerson blandly answers: Why—self-reliance. 'But self-reliance is precisely that secret,—to make your supposed deficiency redundancy. If I am true, the theory is, the very want of action, my very impotency, shall become a greater excellency than all skill and toil.' This from the man who had written, less than a year before, 'Never was anything gained by admitting the omnipotence of limitations, but all immortal action is an overstepping of these busy rules'! Emerson seems to be indulging in some most irresponsible sleight of hand, substituting a small for a capital letter as if the change made no difference and his discovery of the God within had never been.

He thereby makes his early intensities seem more foolish than they deserve; more was at stake than he now admits. Yet by this equivocation he turned the flank of his defeat and saved his faith and his tranquillity.

He found a ready-made route for this retreat on his individuality in the traditional idea of vocation. According to the Protestant ethic that still controlled New England, God called each man to a particular task, and the path of virtue lay in finding one's calling and working in it to the limit of one's power. 'Find Your Calling,' the command of one of his sermons, Emerson himself did his best to fulfill, handicapped as he was by the unconventionality of his course. Since there was no established pattern for him to follow, he had to create his own. As he had written the year before the above lecture, 'Each man has his own vocation. The talent is the call. . . . Every man has this call of the power to do somewhat unique, and no man has any other call.' Henry Nash Smith has shown how much of the trouble in his thoughts, after his break with the church, was due to his need to find his calling, and how the conception of the scholar is the chief one of many attempts to define his vocation.

The attempt was complicated by his simultaneous desire to become a creator in the finite, and so transcend all particular faculties. The only vocation of man, after all, was to be Man. Greatness will not run against obstructions on every side but one; it will know no obstructions on any side. So ran the theory —but experience undermined this hope of totality. '. . . such lobsided, one-eyed half-men are we now, and such a yawning difference between our *esse* and our *posse*.' 'There is no man; there hath never been.' From this *impasse* the idea of vocation offered an escape; if every man is intended to do somewhat unique, he will of course be lobsided. For this reason the ideal of individual uniqueness ran its course in his thought side by side with the ideal of a universal greatness, producing a clash of aims which he frankly acknowledged in 'Nominalist and Realist': 'I assert that every man is a partialist; that nature secures him as an instrument by self-conceit, preventing the tend-

encies to religion and science; . . . and now I add that every man
is a universalist also. . . .'

His Universal Genius called on him to make good his manhood by great action; his individual genius called on him at all
costs to accept his own law. In his journal for 1843 Emerson
argued the whole case of conscience out with himself and ac-
quitted himself of unbelief. 'The two parties in life are the
believers and unbelievers. . . .

'But the unbelief is very profound. Who can escape it? I am
nominally a believer: yet I hold on to property: I eat my bread
with unbelief. . . . My genius loudly calls me to stay where I
am, even with the degradation of owning bank-stock and seeing
poor men suffer, whilst the Universal Genius apprises me of this
disgrace and beckons me to the martyrs [*sic*] and redeemer's
office.

'This is belief, too, this debility of practice, this staying by
our work. For the obedience to a man's genius is the *particular*
of Faith: by and by, shall I come to the *universal* of Faith.' Only
three years later this moral dilemma has dropped entirely out
of sight. 'As the whole has its law, so each individual has his
genius. Obedience to its genius . . . is the particular of faith;
perception that the tendency of the whole is to the benefit of
the individual is the universal of faith.' This revealing change
in the universal of faith neatly illustrates the transference of
the ground of his faith from the Power within to the tendency
of the whole, the transference which underlay his acquiesence.

It had been fear as much as hope that had ever made him feel
that lower-case self-reliance was not enough, a vague dread of
retaliation that had led him to dream of a Self-reliance that
would raise him above all the chances of social hostility and
practical misfortune to a mastery that would be invulnerable
and free. Now, his hope chastened and his basic fear allayed,
he begins to see that 'I dreamed and did not know my dreams.'
Hence the measured farewell to the martyrs and redeemer's
office with which he concluded his lecture on 'New England
Reformers' in 1844. 'Obedience to his genius is the only liberating influence. We wish to escape from subjection and a sense

of inferiority, and we make self-denying ordinances, we drink water, we eat grass, we refuse the laws, we go to jail: it is all in vain; only by obedience to his genius, only by the freest activity in the way constitutional to him, does an angel seem to arise before a man and lead him by the hand out of all the wards of the prison.'

In conspicuous contrast to its closest cognate in the hero-worship of Carlyle, Emerson's cult of greatness had always been democratic. Every man was equal in his potentiality; the Soul in one man was in all others as well. This was a democracy of capacity, noble but impractically ideal. Now he recognized a second democracy of incapacity. If every man was lobsided and unique, then no one could claim dominion over the others. Each individual obeyed his peculiar bias, and universality could be realized only by what we may call the fallacy of rotation. 'The universality being hindered in its primary form, comes in the secondary form of *all sides;* the points come in succession to the meridian, and by the speed of rotation a new whole is formed.' 'Of course it needs the whole society to give the symmetry we seek. The party-colored wheel must revolve very fast to appear white.'

With the mediation of great men removed, Emerson's social philosophy perforce becomes corporate. The alternative was an unthinkable scepticism, a Hobbesian state of nature. Society had to be an organism, in which each individual had his assigned function, even though he himself could not see or understand it. The distribution of the roles, and the coördination of the whole, was the affair of 'the inventor of the game,' and not within man's purview. As this thought sank in, a favorite theme became the habitual insanity of men. Men failed of completeness, not because of a lack or obstruction, but because of an excess. 'Exaggeration is in the course of things. Nature sends no creature, no man into the world without adding a small excess of his proper quality.' 'No man is quite sane; each has a vein of folly in his composition, a slight determination of blood to the head, to make sure of holding him hard to some one point which nature had taken to heart.' The sanity of society was a composite of the counteracting insanities of men, who 'are not philosophers, but are rather very foolish children, who, by reason of their partiality, see everything in the most absurd manner, and are the victims at all times of the nearest object.'

But if society is an organism, composed of foolish children and controlled by some kind of collective soul, what room is there for revolution? Clearly in this context the early vision of a mighty Thinker and Actor who would shatter the forms of society with his new generalization has lost all plausibility.

> Foolish hands may mix and mar;
> Wise and sure the issues are.

Emerson had to accept the skeptic's argument that true character appears, not in heroic rebellion from society, but in a stark and sufficient participation in society; 'his presence supposes a well-ordered society, agriculture, trade, large institutions and empire.' The believer, the skeptic argues in 'Montaigne,' is the conserver. 'We love whatever affirms, connects, preserves; and dislike what scatters or pulls down. . . . Therefore . . . men . . . reject the reformer so long as he comes only with axe and crowbar.' *Natura non facit saltum*. Organisms in nature change only by a slow process of growth; so with society. Part of the change forced by skepticism in Emerson's outlook is the replacement of his evangelical attitude toward social change with an organic and evolutionary point of view. Necessarily, he comes to conceive of the social order, not as a God in ruins that must be rebuilt by some impossible Reformer, but as a single growing entity, in which each pulse of energy, and each following pause, are the successive stages in one evolving process.

Practically, a man was subject to the disposition of necessity, and his chief means of practical freedom was to do the work that came naturally to him. A blind obedience to his native bias, however, was clearly a dubious kind of freedom. As Emerson

had said of heroism, it was unphilosophical, and required a
forfeiture of the claim, so central to his faith, that in union with
the Soul a man shall be informed of all. Viewed from the outside, it was hard to distinguish from the slavery to temperament
which Emerson listed, in 'Experience,' as one of the apparent
facts of life that threatened his faith. So in his second essay
'Nature,' exclusive attention to the principle of Motion in nature, the original impulsion that gives each man his excess of
direction, makes us 'suppose somewhere in the universe a slight
treachery and derision. . . .' But if Motion was one principle
of nature, another was Rest. If man was a partialist, he was a
universalist also; men were not just foolish children, after all,
but philosophers too. Another opposite means of freedom was
to be found in Thought.

'As a ship aground is battered by the waves, so man, imprisoned in mortal life, lies open to the mercy of coming
events. But a truth, separated by the intellect, is no longer a subject of destiny. We behold it as a god upraised above care and
fear.' He had dreamed of transcending care and fear through
an access of practical power that would give him the immunity
of thought without its withdrawal. But the only actual relief he
knew from the pressures of practical life was in his times of
contemplation. What was food for remorse and regret on the
plane of action, on the plane of intellection was matter for
wonder. Even in his time of greatest enthusiasm some part of
him had stood disengaged and aloof, exercising its 'privilege
of Spectatorship,' and answered all interrogations, 'I, oh, I am
only here to see.'

Seeing, as well as doing, of course, was a main ambition for
him from the start—naturally so, since he was by nature essentially a watcher. Side by side with his ethical and practical
aspirations, and temperamentally more real to him, we find an
alternative endeavor to reach freedom through thought. The
great emancipating privilege of contemplation was the sight of
God through Reason, or better, the union with God, since the
mind's 'vision is not like the vision of the eye, but is union
with the things known.' A typical instance is the sylvan rapture

described in *Nature:* 'I become a transparent eyeball; I am doing nothing; I see all; the currents of the Universal Being circulate through me; I am part or parcel of God.' Salvation by action meant a heroism that could conquer and prevail over appearances. Salvation by thought meant a detachment from the seeming reality of appearances through a union with the Cause.

This sort of rapt repudiation of the outer world for the Soul was a powerful recurrent movement in Emerson's spirit, in his earlier as in his later years. From the coil of anxiety and constraint and puzzlement and cross-purposes of his life with men, he repeatedly retreated with profound relief to communion with the Soul within and shook the dust of earth from his feet. This was the thrill of idealism for him, that it could 'dissipate this block of earth into shining ether,' and release him into a Godlike solitude in which 'the world itself loses its solidity, nothing remains but the soul and the Divine Presence in which it lives.'

'The things we now esteem fixed shall, one by one, detach themselves like ripe fruit from our experience, and fall. The wind shall blow them none knows whither. The landscape, the figures, Boston, London, are facts as fugitive as any institution past, or any whiff of mist or smoke, and so is society, and so is the world. The soul looketh steadily forwards, creating a world before her, leaving worlds behind her. She has no dates, nor rites, nor persons, nor specialties, nor men. The soul knows only the soul. . . .' I know nothing in literature that carries quite this measured chill, as if a voice from outer space had pronounced upon all human enterprise. One thinks again of *The Mysterious Stranger*, but Satan there ventriloquizes a bitter disillusion that is absent here. Perhaps the closest modern spirit, though it seems strange to say so, is T. S. Eliot.

> . . . the strained time-ridden faces
> Distracted from distraction by distraction
> Filled with fancies and empty of meaning
> Tumid apathy with no concentration
> Men and bits of paper, whirled by the cold wind . .
> Driven on the wind that sweeps the gloomy hills of London,

Hampstead and Clerkenwell, Campden and Putney,
Highgate, Primrose and Ludgate. . . .[8]

But Eliot does not greet the discovery that ordinary life is no
more than a whiff of smoke, or a bit of paper before the wind,
with Emerson's Olympian consent. In moments such as these,
Emerson enters an upper region where the atmosphere is almost
too rarefied for mortal lungs.

The hour of vision, in which 'The soul raised over passion . . . calms itself with knowing that all things go well,'
was the unique privilege of the thinker. Yet, as is plain, contemplation had its limitations and dangers, too, which prevented
Emerson from ever turning to a steady cultivation of a mystical
death to the world as a solution to his problems.

One of these was what he called in 'Montaigne' the levity
of intellect. The saintly rejection of the world for the Spirit
blended imperceptibly into another state of mind much less
visibly holy, whose attraction had much to do with his willing-
ness to retreat to the Soul, and yet which repelled him too. For
the ground of this kind of victory over the world was not, as
in the imagined case of the hero, a conquering will, but a withdrawal from the field. His vision of the Soul raised him above
concern with his mortal circumstances. In the security thus
granted he could turn back and overlook the world, contem-
plating the queer tangle of mortal life, and even his own shortcomings, with the equanimity of a spectator.

This technique of victory by disengagement he spelled out in
a journal entry of 1837: 'The victory is won as soon as any
Soul has learned always to take sides with Reason against himself; to transfer his Me from his person, his name, his interest,
back upon Truth and Justice, so that when he is disgraced and
defeated and fretted and disheartened, and wasted by nothings,
he bears it well, never one instant relaxing his watchfulness,
and, as soon as he can get a respite from the insults or the sad-

---

[8] T. S. Eliot, *Four Quartets* (New York: Harcourt, Brace and Co., 1943),
p. 6.

ness, records all these phenomena, pierces their beauty as phenomena, and, like a God, oversees himself. . . . Keep the habit of
the observer, and, as fast as you can, break off your association
with your personality and identify yourself with the Universe.
Be a football to Time and Chance, the more kicks, the better,
so that you inspect the whole game and know its uttermost law.'
In this way, he added, he could be a 'winning loser.' To cultivate
the habit of the observer therefore became a regular recourse
as his hopes of mastery faded.

It seems clear that he would have been much less willing to
accept the detachment of thought than he was, whatever his
personal needs, if his faith in the Soul had not allowed him to
think of the solitude of thought as a higher companionship
with the Soul. But the observer's trick of inspecting the whole
game was something other than a devotion to the Soul: indeed,
the Soul as well as the world could and did become only one
more object of his passionless vision. It was a self-disconnection
from the whole life of emotion. Emerson felt the loss of humanity, as did Hawthorne, in a life of pure observation.

With him, it was not so much the death of the heart that
disturbed him, as the detachment from morals. There was a
high-level conflict between insight and holiness; they ought to
be unanimous, but experience did not find them so. So the
saint's discovery of the Universal, in the lecture on 'Holiness,'
was treated entirely as a practical surrender to the moral sentiment rather than an hour of vision, though it was a religious
intuition that made this ethical inspiration possible. Even in
his discourses at Harvard on the 'Natural History of Intellect,'
which were put together in the 1870's, the two modes of the
Soul, truth and moral sentiment, both reappear, no nearer a
reconciliation. A conviction that the intuitions of the Soul
which visited his thoughts were, or ought to be, at the same time
intimations of a renewed virtue strongly checked his natural
drift toward a life of contemplation.

A related danger in contemplation sprang from the impermanence of his moments of vision. The obverse of such revelations, as his skeptical essays made plain, was illusion, which

may be defined in this connection as idealism without the vision of the Ideal. A sense of illusion—a knowledge of the unreality of this world, and a lack of present experience of a greater reality—was the penalty he paid for the decision to sit at home with the Cause, one that recurred more and more to plague him as his capacity for enthusiastic vision dwindled with time. Then, like his skeptic, he was likely to rebel against his unreal life of thought altogether. Appropriately, illusion became one of the main grounds for the skeptic's doubts.[4]

❦

One could not, after all, live only by mere seeing, any more than by mere doing. Both freedom through working in one's vocation, and freedom through beholding, were partial and limited. If the first was unphilosophical, the second was irresponsible. At best, some sort of working freedom could be achieved by alternating them, and this seems in fact to have been his best practical answer to the problem. As he early discovered, the active and the intellectual powers seemed to be naturally governed by a principle of undulation; his life moved with a certain regular rhythm from one to the other. The closest he came to combining them in theory was in his portrait of his final vocational hero-type, the Poet.

The poet was neither Knower nor Doer, but Sayer. Undeniably there was some limitation here—a relinquished hope of power. '. . . Nature . . . wished [Poets] to stand for the Intellect and not for the Will. . . .' Perhaps in some future incarnation 'this genius who today can upheave . . . every object in nature for his metaphor' will be 'capable . . . of playing such a game with his hands instead of his brain.' Emerson had not forgotten what he wrote in 1836, when discussing the fine arts, for which he had less feeling: 'There is higher work for Art than the arts. They are abortive births of an imperfect or vitiated instinct. Art is the need to create; but . . . Nothing less than the creation of man and nature is its end.'

[4] See pp. 113-17.

But these reservations, which one would expect to play an important part in his estimate of the poet's vocation, dwindle to nothing in comparison with the rhapsodic praise the poet receives, in verse and prose, in the 1840's. 'He is the man whose being soars higher and sinks deeper than another's, to a softer tenderness, a holier ardor, a grander daring. This is the man who makes all other men seem less, the very naming of whose name is ornamental and like good news, and the sound of his words for ages makes the heart beat quicker, and the eye glisten, and fills the air with golden dreams,' etc., etc. The very fact that he is not a doer increases his prestige. Emerson exploits the Platonic tradition of the poet's madness. A man possessed, he is exempt from the ordinary human responsibility to be of use; no failure to act can be held against him. A born rhapsodist, his one duty is to mind his rhyme. For this reason, one may suspect, after 1840, he overshadows all other hero-types in Emerson's gallery of ideals. What would be limitation in anyone else is irrelevance to him.

Certainly there is no admission of limitation in Emerson's portrait of the poet. 'He is a sovereign, and stands on the centre.' 'The poet is . . . the man without impediment, who sees and handles that which others dream of, traverses the whole scale of experience, and is representative of man, in virtue of being the largest power to receive and to impart.' His saying *is* action: 'Words and deeds are quite indifferent modes of the divine energy. Words are also actions, and actions are a kind of words.' All men, as they receive, so they crave to express; the release of energy is a need of nature. Utterance in this inclusive sense may even be the end of man. 'A man should know himself for a necessary actor. A link was wanting between two craving parts of nature, and he was hurled into being as the bridge over that yawning need, the mediator betwixt two else unmarriageable facts. . . . The thoughts he delights to utter are the reason of his incarnation.' This deliverance the poet performs best, and thus 'He stands among partial men for the complete man. . . .' Saying *includes* knowing and doing.

The poet is the only liberator. Through his poems the ideal

can become for a moment real; 'one golden word leaps out immortal . . . and sweetly torments us with invitations to its own inaccessible homes.' He alone can in any sense abdicate a manifold and duplex life. 'And this is the reward,' Emerson tells his poet; 'that the ideal shall be real to thee, and the impressions of the actual world shall fall like summer rain, copious, but not troublesome to thy invulnerable essence.'

In placing the poet at the center Emerson was being no more than true to his own experience; the poet was certainly *his* representative man. In a vocational ideal, which was in all essential respects a giant shadow of himself, a portrait of what he would truly like to be, he restored to himself in some measure the possibility of manhood, of which in a universal and unlimited sense he had despaired. And yet we can see that the victory of the poet presupposes the earlier defeat. It is only because the poetic *life* is not realized, perhaps cannot be, that the poet's *prophecy* of such a life can make him a liberating god. If we could realize the ideal in life, it would not be such a service to realize it in words. The poet's own liberation is a liberation of the intellect. The poet's life is not a poetic life, but an ascetic service of his thought. His reward, the reward he brings others, is not self-union, but a magic flare of imagination, without means and without issue, an intoxicating glimpse of the inaccessible ideal.

The poet is Uriel lapsed, withdrawn behind his cloud. He is the chief of the truth-speaking things which, by hints and symbols, can shake the world with premonitions of a higher truth. Failing to command the power to persuade and convert directly, Emerson looks for the means of masked communication. Yet he has to add, 'I look in vain for the poet whom I describe.' This pattern also is too big for human nature—certainly for his own powers. Uriel is a god, for whom of course the ideal is the real. But for a mortal, in spite of occasional poetic glimpses, they remain in indissoluble contradiction. Emerson's actual work, then, was less that of a liberating god than that of 'a faithful reporter of particular impressions.' 'I write Metaphysics, but my method is purely expectant. It is not even tentative. Much

less am I ingenious in instituting *experimenta crucis* to extort
the secret and lay bare the reluctant lurking law. No, I confine
my ambition to true reporting, though I only get one new fact
in a year.' For the writer, as for the man, a palpable gap, which
nothing could close, lay between what he might be and what
he was.

Freedom, as he argued in his essay 'Fate,' is a fact of experience, never to be denied—but not the total freedom he had once
claimed as the birthright of the scholar. Man's freedom, like
everything else in human life, is limited and partial; behind it,
including it, is necessity. He could remain peaceful and satisfied
enough, however, for all his limitations, because of his larger
generalization. The mystic identity of the ideal and the real,
though contradicted by all experience, was still revealed to
him in the hours of clear reason. During the rest of time, when
he could not disassociate himself from his mortal condition and
live in the mind alone, when consequently true reporting was
his only work, and a Stoic fidelity to duty his only ethics, he
derived his courage to live from a trust in *'the eternal tendency
to the good of the whole, active in every atom, every moment'*
(Emerson's italics). In this larger good his own mixed fortunes
could be swallowed up and forgotten.

In 1837, Emerson had written America's 'intellectual Declaration of Independence,' *The American Scholar.* Seven years later
he returned to the theme of American destiny in 'The Young
American,' and this time we get a larger generalization. 'Gentlemen, there is a sublime and friendly Destiny by which the
human race is guided,—the race never dying, the individual
never spared,—to results affecting masses and ages. Men are
narrow and selfish, but the Genius or Destiny is not narrow,
but beneficent. It is not discovered in their calculated and voluntary activity, but in what befalls, with or without their design.
Only what is inevitable interests us, and it turns out that love
and good are inevitable, and in the course of things.'

The same address emphasizes the individual powerlessness
which gave the beneficent tendency its importance. 'This Genius
or Destiny is of the sternest administration, though rumors

exist of its secret tenderness. It may be styled a cruel kindness, serving the whole even to the ruin of the member; a terrible communist, reserving all profits to the community, without dividend to individuals. Its law is, you shall have everything as a member, nothing to yourself.' A strange encouragement to offer a still Jacksonian America! Although Emerson often rather blurred this distinction of whole and member and less critically asserted a faith in Goodness in general, the passage illustrates all the better the quality of his acquiesence. Though balanced by an emerging humanism that continued to stress man's freedom for self-improvement, it implies, as the ground of his confidence, the unconditional surrender of his first radical egoism. There is more than a suggestion in it of the 'consistent Calvinist's' 'Are you willing to be damned for the glory of God?' Emerson's ancestrally inspired humility swallows up his pride.

CHAPTER EIGHT

The Eternal Pan

E MERSON'S submission to a sublime and friendly Destiny grew up in his mind in close association with a changed attitude toward nature, one which went hand in hand with his whole shift away from egoism, and which so altered the context and atmosphere of his religious thought that a trust in the tendency of things as they are became the only plausible form for his faith to take. Originally he thought of the Soul as within the self; nature was an exteriorization of this aboriginal Self, was even in a transcendental sense man's creation. Now, rather, he thought of the Soul as within nature, and of man as her late, if supreme, product. As a part of nature, man shared in the Soul; as the only conscious part of nature, he even had the special privilege to see and know the Soul within him; but he was no longer prior to or apart from the world around him. Emerson moved from a subjective toward an objective idealism.

The cause of this shift was not so much the collapse of his dream of Self-reliance, as it was the entrance into his thought of a new way of conceiving nature, the general idea of evolution. In dealing with Emerson we must understand the term very loosely. It does not imply a Darwinian belief in the transmutation of species by natural selection, but simply 'a series of events in chronological sequence; life being regarded historically as later in appearance than inorganic matter, and the higher forms of life as following the lower in a graduated scale of ascent.' Behind and through the natural sequence worked the same higher Cause. 'The question . . . whether the trilobites, or whether the gods, are our grandfathers . . . arises from the contingence whether we look from the material or from the poetic side.' 'The faithful dogma assumes that the other is an optical show, but that the Universe was long already complete through law. . . .'

He did not come to the thought of evolution all at once. F. I. Carpenter has remarked on the slowness with which new ideas seeped down into the roots of Emerson's thinking. It took him many years of reading in the Asiatics before his thought began to show an Oriental tinge, and similarly evolution had been a familiar idea to him long before it began really to affect his point of view. An anthropocentric philosophy characterizes his first book, *Nature;* the evolutionary motto of that book was not added until the second edition in 1849. By a slow process of seepage, however, he came by insensible degrees to accept the idea of a constant metamorphosis and progression in nature.

Yet we should notice that he continues to insist on the centrality of man in nature. If man is not her creator, he is her climax and end. In 1841, when the new way of conceiving nature was beginning to take effect, he could write, 'The termination of the world in a man appears to be the last victory of intelligence.' In 1844, when it had become pretty well established, he continued to assert that 'we traverse the whole scale of being, from the centre to the poles of nature, and have some stake in every possibility. . . .' So ten years later he spoke of the whole animal world as 'only a Hunterian museum to exhibit the genesis of mankind.'

Even the passage which has been called 'the most uncompromising declaration Emerson was ever to make that man is a child of earth' is a commentary on two lines from Herbert's 'Man'—a poem which makes the opposite declaration—and is after all not so very uncompromising. 'The master can do his great deed, the desire of the world, . . . because he has just come out of Nature, or from being a part of that thing. . . . He knows the laws of azote because just now he was azote. Man is only a piece of the universe made alive. Man active can do what just now he suffered.' The implications of this passage are perhaps more striking to the seeker after evolutionary passages in Emerson than its main purpose—to support his old theme of man's related nature—really warrants. The concept of evolution typically figures in his mind as a new support for his old assertion of man's key position in nature.

In two chief ways, however, the idea of evolution figured in the evolution of his thought. For one thing, it helped to account for the gap between royal man as he should be, and the universal rottenness of man as he was.

> There lives no man of Nature's worth
> In the circle of the earth. . . .

This exception to the perfect order of nature was, as Gray has pointed out, the great anomaly in his faith. He tried to account for it in *Nature*, in the Platonic manner, by a myth of a 'lapse'; the fact remained disconcerting and unaccountable. But with the growth of an evolutionary concept of nature, the facts became more intelligible. One need only assume that the process of evolution is not yet complete. To the question 'whether the experiment have not failed, and whether it be quite worth while to make more [men], and glut the innocent space with so poor an article'—to this nature replies (in 'The Method of Nature'): ' "I grow." All is nascent, infant. . . . We can point nowhere to anything final; but tendency appears on all hands: planet, system, constellation, total nature is growing like a field of maize in July; is becoming somewhat else; is in rapid metamorphosis.'

A general melioristic confidence about the future perceptibly seeps into his later thought, a confidence of which the growth of his faith in a benevolent tendency is symptomatic. In this way he partially regains what the collapse of his transcendentalism seemed to have lost. Originally he could reconcile present limitation with potential divinity because he considered the first temporary; the future would bring the reconciliation. With time this expectation evaporated, and he was left with the unmitigated contradiction of fact and faith. This dilemma the notion of evolution alleviated. It restored to him the vision of a future reconciliation of his two worlds—now nothing so personal or immediate as his first hopes, but still a *pou sto* for his faith. '. . . if evil is good in the making, if limitation is power that shall be, if calamities, oppositions, and weights are wings and means,—we are reconciled.' Because of this belief he is not constrained to accept an unconditional surrender to the will of

God but can soften his submission with the comfortable thought that the divine energy is

> Without halting, without rest,
> Lifting Better up to Best. . . .

The idea of evolution also had an effect of a deeper sort—to reinforce his sense of the universal flux of things, and at the same time of the pervasiveness of law. At the time of *Nature*, though he spoke of nature's floods of life, his conception of nature was static and material. Nature was the last issue of spirit. 'In the divine order, intellect is primary; nature, secondary; it is the memory of the mind. That which once existed in intellect as pure law, has now taken body as Nature.' Spirit was embodied in an infinite variety of forms, whose unity in variety conspicuously illustrated nature's submission to laws and tempted the curiosity of the naturalist. But there was no implication that there was metamorphosis among these forms, and the basic characteristic of nature remained her materiality.

Evolution almost literally dissolved this conception of nature. Both form and matter lost their final character and began to flow. At the heart of nature, where before he had seen a matter opposed to life, he now saw vitality and change. But this dissolution of the present order of nature only strengthened his belief in her governing laws. With the loss of other stability, these became the only principle of permanence left.

Evolution came to him as a grand simplifying and unifying idea, a comprehensive principle for interpreting nature; it removed what resistance he had felt to the idea of her infinite variety by providing a dramatic demonstration of a guiding unity behind it. Her increased diversity was lost in the all-inclusive unity of the idea of progressive development. This sense of an incessant flux in nature, and yet of a guiding identity behind it, is the most conspicuous theme of 'The Method of Nature' and of the second essay 'Nature,' and is the real point of the passage from 'Poetry and Imagination' quoted by Joseph Warren Beach as the sum of his philosophy of nature.

First innuendoes, then broad hints, then smart taps are given, suggesting that nothing stands still in Nature but death; that the creation is on wheels, in transit, always passing into something else, streaming into something higher; that matter is not what it appears.
. . . Thin or solid, everything is in flight. . . . and nothing fast but those invisible cords which we call laws, on which all is strung. . . . the secret cords or laws show their well-known virtue through every variety, be it animal, or plant, or planet. . . .

Identity of law, perfect order in physics, perfect parallelism between the laws of Nature and the laws of thought exist. . . .

There is one animal, one plant, one matter and one force.

～

Perhaps too much attention has been paid in discussions of Emerson's idea of evolution to the narrow question of the time-relation of the species. This matter really did not concern him much; yet we still cannot fail to see that a change did take place in his thought of nature that transformed its whole context and atmosphere. This change was instigated not so much by the strict thought of evolution as by Emerson's reading in geology.
Though he had been long familiar with the uniformitarian theories of Hutton and Playfair, it was particularly Lyell that set him off. He read Lyell about 1836; and about that time a new note slips into his forest thoughts. It spoke of 'archaic calendars of the sun and the internal fire, of the wash of rivers and oceans for durations inconceivable'; of 'Chimborazo and Mont Blanc and Himmaleh,' of the 'silent procession of brute elements.' A sense of the undreamed-of immensity and brute violence of the processes of nature grows up in his imagination.
' "Miracles have ceased." Have they indeed? . . . Tell me, good friend, when this hillock on which your foot stands swelled from the level of the sphere by volcanic force; pick up that pebble at your foot; look at its gray sides, its sharp crystal, and tell me what fiery inundation of the world melted the minerals like wax, and, as if the globe were one glowing crucible, gave this stone its shape. . . . Why cannot geology, why cannot botany speak and tell me what has been, what is, as I run along the

forest promontory, and ask when it rose like a blister on heated
steel?'

The domestic nature of his youth, the kitchen-garden of the
Soul, has expanded with Gothic sublimity into something very
much vaster and stranger. The affinity to his own mind of the
forces that control her seems suddenly less obvious. And above
all the effect of his reading in geology is to open up for him a
dizzy perspective into the dark backward and abysm of time.
'Geology has initiated us into the secularity of nature, and taught
us to disuse our dame-school measure, and exchange our Mosaic
and Ptolemaic schemes for her large style. We knew nothing
rightly, for want of perspective. Now we learn what patient
periods must round themselves before the rock is formed; then
before the rock is broken, and the first lichen race has disin-
tegrated the thinnest external plate into soil, and opened the
door for the remote Flora, Fauna, Ceres, and Pomona to come
in. How far off yet is the trilobite! how far the quadruped! how
inconceivably remote is man!'

It is this enlarged conception of nature that does most to
throw his first egocentric transcendentalism into a new perspective. In the light of the nature revealed by geology the ridiculous
arrogance of such egoism is patent. Nature is something too
vast, too long-lived, too powerful and too alien to be subordi-
nated to the mere individual. This changed perspective lies behind his revival in his second essay 'Nature' of the scholastic
distinction, via Coleridge, between *natura naturata* and *natura
naturans*. The first is the familiar nature of the senses, the woods
and the fields. But the second stands in the place occupied in
Nature by 'Spirit' and seems indistinguishable from God. It is
'Efficient Nature, *natura naturans,* the quick cause before which
all forms flee as the driven snows; itself secret, its works driven
before it in flocks and multitudes, . . . and in undescribable
variety.' The rest of the essay discusses a nature which has become another name for the Cause.

A faith in Efficient Nature, however, acted as an alternative
for, but did not replace, Emerson's first faith in the humanity
of the Soul. Nature was, after all, the NOT ME, and her worship

threatened to subject him to a power alien to himself. He preferred to distinguish Spirit both from nature and man, as the need arose, and to worship Reality directly, in its own name. Yet that his faith in nature could on occasion satisfy his religious impulses is demonstrated by the address on 'The Method of Nature.'

The address, to be sure, is one of his most inconsistent writings. The root of the trouble seems to be, to state it briefly, that the address, contemporary with his essay 'Circles,' represents an incomplete stage in his assimilation of his new conception of nature, so that in it he still tries to derive the old anthropocentric lessons of *Nature* from his new nature of flux and evolution. Yet the new vision of flowing nature here, through which, as Cabot has suggested, we can hear the note of the ocean beside which, at Nantasket, he composed part of the address, lifts him to an unusual peak of faith.

His consciousness of the unseizable flux of nature serves to heighten his sense of the metaphysical spring of her vitality. We are unable, he argues, to read the secret of nature because she is not to be understood by intellect. Nature has no particular cause, no particular end. She has her cause in her own boundless life, and her end is ecstasy. Ever-renewed nature, felt as a whole, speaks of an overflowing principle of Life as her cause which is not to be known but can be felt and loved.

How silent, how spacious, what room for all, yet without place to insert an atom;—in graceful succession, in equal fulness, in balanced beauty, the dance of the hours goes forward still. Like an odor of incense, like a strain of music, like a sleep, it is inexact and boundless. It will not be dissected, nor unravelled, nor shown. Away, profane philosopher! seekest thou in nature the cause? This refers to that, and that to the next, and the next to the third, and everything refers. Thou must ask in another mood, thou must feel it and love it, thou must behold it in a spirit as grand as that by which it exists, ere thou canst know the law. Known it will not be, but gladly beloved and enjoyed.

In this mood of exalted confidence, Emerson transcends the barrier the new flux of nature puts in the path of his old faith.

Nature is not to be understood; she is a ceaseless flow of life, an immortal energy. Faith is an ecstasy in which man immerses himself in this stream of life. Newly aware of the vast spending of things, not yet settled in the consciousness of his human limitations, Emerson responds with a powerful sense of release to the idea of a possible union *by love alone* to the currents of being. This, perhaps, is the secret of freedom—to break away from endless speculation, abandon all philosophy, and approach the throne through the heart. The debate of truth and love is a recurrent theme in Emerson, generally decided in theory by an assertion of their identity, in practice in favor of truth. Here for once he goes over to the anti-intellectual side. The result is that the Gordian knot of his metaphysical riddles is momentarily cut, and he comes for the time to a real consummation. Though no such ecstasy, of course, could endure, the pure joy of this moment of release carries over into his writing and makes parts of this address memorable among his writings on nature.

To feel and love the creative energy in nature, however, is a treacherous mode of worship. 'Nature is a stranger yet,' as Emily Dickinson was to write.

> To pity those that know her not
> Is helped by the regret
> That those who know her, know her less
> The nearer her they get.

Nature indeed is power, but how do we know she is beneficent? The worship of energy because it is so energetic is, as Santayana called it, barbarism. At any moment one may, like Melville and Adams, burst through the rotten flooring of this kind of faith and drop into the 'religious void' beneath.

Nevertheless, such a worship of vital force strongly drew Emerson's imagination. He had always balanced his vision of a nature saturated with law with a vivid sense of nature's floods of life, and his admiration of a greatness in the might of the moral sentiment with an envy of the wild virtue of the man who can do things. 'Not out of those on whom systems of education have exhausted their culture, comes the helpful giant to destroy the old or to build the new, but out of unhandselled savage nature; out of terrible Druids and Berserkers come at last Alfred and Shakspeare.' In the same spirit this pale scholar showed a relish for 'the conversation of a strong-natured farmer or backwoodsman,' and questioned 'whether we have not lost by refinement some energy, by a Christianity, entrenched in establishments and forms, some vigor of wild virtue.' Like Thoreau, he balanced his devotion to holiness ('higher laws') with a taste for wildness. 'Wild man attracts. . . . but men in society do not interest us because they are tame.'

At the time of his lecture series on *Biography* his belief in the spirituality of power was dominant. Power resulted from an influx of the religious sentiment, in whose strength a man might confront even 'the unintelligent brute force that lies at the bottom of society.' But we have watched him come to suspect that power was rather a natural gift, more the product of animal spirits than of a divine inspiration. As a result (while he continued to assert a belief in the moral sentiment and the unlimited power it brought with it) the creative power in the universe, and the human power to act that derived from it, lost many of their spiritual and moral associations for him and coalesced in his mind rather with the aboriginal force of unhandselled savage nature.

The tendency grows, therefore, in his later thought, though not without heavy qualification—an example is his essay 'Power' in *The Conduct of Life*—to equate all manifestations of power as so many modes of the divine energy. Though power can be raw and crude, it is the stuff of life. A man is strong only as he participates in this; without it, he must be shallow and unsatisfying. The bestial energy of the mob, of the savage, is after all their divine side, since it springs from this dread origin. To be sure, man must progress from blind force to accuracy, to skill, to truth, but he degenerates when his refinement has cut him off from this brute youth. 'In history the great moment is when the savage is just ceasing to be a savage. . . . Everything good in nature and the world is in that moment of transition, when the swarthy juices still flow plentifully from nature, but their astringency or acridity is got out by ethics and humanity.'

And beyond the practical manifestations of power lay the vision of the quick Cause. If one pole of Emerson's later worship was a submission to law and benevolent tendency, another became his awe and entranced surrender at the spectacle of nature's vast creative power. The feeling-tone of this mode of his worship has been well described by Joseph Warren Beach: 'It relieves the strain on our individual conscience to realize how infinitesimal a part we play in the drama of the ages. Our anxious distinctions of good and evil grow vague and petty in the perspective of eternity. And at the same time our hearts are lifted up with the consciousness that we are part and parcel of the universal, the august and infallible Spirit.'

One feeling that lifted up Emerson's heart, I would suggest, was a thrill of danger. This was a much less reassuring interpretation of the nature revealed by geology and evolution than was the notion of a benevolent tendency, and it gave his confidence in the good intentions of his universe a run for its money. If the forward look up the evolutionary scale encouraged melioristic confidence, the backward glance at nature's secular growth could bring a shudder at the Abyss out of which all had come. In what inconceivable Nox and Chaos had evolution begun!—untamed energy, savage power, which it was still the far-from-completed labor of Melioration to refine. Nature *was* other, was a ruthless energy little concerned with the fortunes of one individual more or less. The thought was hardly friendly to his need of beneficence, a sobering glimpse of the 'terror at the heart of worship' which recalls Melville. He could no longer be nearly as sure as when celebrating the Over-Soul in 1840 that 'his welfare is dear to the heart of being.' Beneath the trust in nature's beneficence lies the sense of 'a deeper cause, as yet far from being conscious.'

This is the tendency in his thought that responded to his readings in Oriental, particularly Buddhist, literature, perhaps also, as Gray suggests, to echoes reaching him of Schelling's Identity-philosophy. As Carpenter and Christy have shown, Emerson's readings in Buddhism did not begin to 'take' until nearly 1846; the frequency of references after that indicate the depth of their influence then on his thought. The force of that influence was to cut under the lingering anthropomorphism of his deity, and the deity's too close association with the supposed benevolence of nature, and to suggest instead an unknown, unnamable One behind appearances, a substance older and deeper than mind and matter, indifferent to all human values, the identity of all things yet identical with nothing, 'a deaf, unimplorable, immense fate.' 'The Indian system is full of fate . . . it is the dread reality, it is the cropping-out in our planted gardens of the core of the world: it is the abysmal Force, untameable and immense.'

The universal identity of things, their unity in Brahma, before which all notion of individual freedom vanishes, was what Emerson felt Asia above all had to teach him. This was a grand conception, but also inhuman. By religion, man tends to unity— to rise above his personal life and merge himself with the One. But 'Nature will not be Buddhist.' So his praise of Plato, the balanced soul, is based on his ability to synthesize the two poles of life, the One and the Many, Asia and Europe, thought and action—the necessary duality of human life. 'The middle region of our being is the temperate zone.'

Yet in certain moods Buddhism had a powerful appeal. More perfectly than any less extreme thought, it made possible for him the relief of an utter submission. He could compensate for the undermining of his original egoism by throwing himself altogether the other way and transcending all false secondary distinctions in a self-identification with this omnipresent One. 'I am of the Maker and of the Made. The vastness of the Universe, the portentous year of Mizar and Alcor are no vastness, no longevity to me. . . . Through all the running sea of forms, I am truth, I am love, and immutable I transcend form as I do time and space.'

The best-known expression of this strain in his thought is his poem 'Brahma.' It is, indeed, a theme for which he generally chose the more rhapsodic speech of poetry. This is

> The over-god
> Who marries Right to Might,
>
> .   .   .   .   .   .
>
> He who exterminates
> Races by stronger races,
> Black by white faces,—

of the 'Ode' to Channing; this is the 'World-Soul'—

> Love-without-weakness,—
>
> .   .   .   .   .   .
>
> He kills the cripple and the sick,
> And straight begins again . . . .

Something similar, as Professor Beach points out, crops up at the conclusion and climax of 'Woodnotes.'

> Onward and on, the eternal Pan,
> Who layeth the world's incessant plan,
> Halteth never in one shape,
> But forever doth escape,
> Like wave or flame, into new forms
> Of gem, and air, of plants, and worms.
>
> .   .   .   .   .   .
>
> Alike to him the better, the worse,—
> The glowing angel, the outcast corse.
> Thou metest him by centuries,
> And lo! he passes like the breeze;
> Thou seek'st in globe and galaxy,
> He hides in pure transparency;
> Thou askest in fountains and in fires,
> He is the essence that inquires.
> He is the axis of the star;
> He is the sparkle of the spar;
> He is the heart of every creature;
> He is the meaning of each feature;
> And his mind is the sky.
> Than all it holds more deep, more high.

Again, there is more than a little suggestion here and in 'Brahma,' domesticating his Orientalism, of the old Puritan submission before the searing flame of God's naked power. 'The Power that deals with us . . . is, in sum, dazzling, terrific, inaccessible.'

Thus Emerson on the one hand protected himself from the sense of powerlessness involved in his acquiescence by leaning on the benevolent tendency of the universe. Yet also his reading in geology and in the Hindus takes effect in a new awareness of the space between the law and the searing flame, and, as a counterstatement to this excess of sweetness, there rises something like the ancestral awe before the dazzling, terrific, inaccessible power of the Almighty.

CHAPTER NINE

The Old Scholar

MY CREED is very simple,' Emerson wrote in 1841, 'that Goodness is the only Reality, that to Goodness alone can we trust, to that we may trust all and always; beautiful and blessed and blessing is it, even though it should seem to slay me.

'Beyond this I have no knowledge, no intelligence of methods; I know no steps, no degrees, no favorite means, no detached rules. Itself is gate and road and leader and march. Only trust it, be of it, be it, and it shall be well with us forever. It will be and govern in its own transcendent way, and not in ways that arithmetic and mortal experience can measure.'

To such agnostic optimism finally simmered down the glorious hopes of his transcendental decade. Already well formed by the publication of his *Essays, Second Series,* in 1844, it was his settled position by the time he left America for the second time to make a lecture tour of England. This second trip abroad may be conveniently taken to mark the conclusion of the real development of his thought. Up to 1848 was in a broad sense his seminal period; from then on he reaped the harvest of wisdom.

We no longer find in his later books either the confusion or the dramatic uncertainty that accompanied the serious adjustments of his earlier thought. The transcendental issue, the crucial question of his early inner life, had been decided; his optimism, immune to experience, had no power of further growth; and now, secure in the arms of the Wise God, nothing remained but to fulfill his vocation and while away his time on earth by drawing the portrait of such lords of life as he could distinguish and by charting the conditions of mortal life and happiness. In this enterprise he shows admirable scope and balance, and an increased sureness and clarity; his social frame of reference, as Robert E. Spiller points out, markedly expands;

154

he has lost only, if it be a loss, a certain sense of unpredictable possibilities, a feeling of immeasurable hope, which gave his earlier writings, in contrast to his later, an air of high romance.

The presiding deity in his journals after 1848 remains nature. Nature is the whole of which his particular truths are somehow parts; man's present condition is a stage in her vast process. As his personal force diminishes, the thought of nature's power, and a faith in her tendency, sustains him to run his course. To report man's place in nature's holy plan becomes his chief vocation.

Underlying all is the 'power of Fate, the dynastic oppression of Submind.' He now accepts the plain fact that most souls belong to the world of fate, or animal good. Their fixed determinations are the very means by which high nature works. Free souls are rare, and even in them inheres an old inertia which punishes, as it were, any fit of geniality. Only once in five hundred years, perhaps, comes a hero, to realize one specialty of the promise of the mind. A leading note of his later journals is a rueful acknowledgment of the enlarging role of trivialities in the daily life of the old scholar. 'To-day, carpets; yesterday, the aunts; the day before, the funeral of poor S.; and every day, the remembrance in the library of the rope of work which I must spin;—in this way life is dragged down and confuted. We try to listen to the hymn of gods, and must needs hear this perpetual *cock-a-doodle-doo*, and *ke-tar-kut* right under the library windows.'

Yet we can make no greater mistake than to describe his attitude in these harvest years as merely a helpless submission to a disposing fate. Deepening the smile of benign acquiescence with which he met the fact of necessity was the satisfaction of an old campaigner at the prospect of a good fight under fair auspices. Man's latent power was never clearer to him than when the mirage of total victory no longer engrossed his sight. The privilege still of at least some favored men was to cut loose from nature's determinations and become self-directing agents. Emerson's scorn of the many-too-many measurably increased—though it never became absolute—as time diminished his belief in men's equal openness to inspiration, and he recognized the dependence of social progress on 'a few competent heads.' Now he put his faith in the natural aristocrat.

'With culture . . . the self-direction develops.' One ally of the well-born man in his self-liberation is refinement, from the discipline of good manners to the cultivation of the intellect and the moral nature. Though, as his comments on England show, mere material progress impresses Emerson little more than it did Carlyle, he has lost his original hostility to the influence of organized society on the natural man. Man is amphibious, 'with one door down into Tartarus, and one door upward into light, belonging to both'; he is perfected as he mounts, by civilization, from his savage beginnings to light. The task of the modern era is 'to marry mind to Nature, and to put Nature under the mind. . . .'

The key thought of this time, however, is that man, in putting nature under mind, has nature for an ally. The state to which man subject to nature aspires is a higher state of nature, an 'identification of the Ego with the universe'; through nature, nature is conquered. '. . . all we value,' he wrote in 1857, 'is the *naturel,* or peculiar quality of each man,' which is both the antagonist and the next finer ascent or metamorphosis of 'gravitation, vegetation, chemistry.' 'But the essence of it is, that it be native and intuitive.'

We must discriminate fate from the necessary, he explained in a careful statement of his position in May 1859. '. . . Fate is the name we give to the action of that one eternal, all-various necessity on the brute myriads, whether in things, animals, or in men in whom the intellect pore is not yet opened.' But with 'the birth of perception,' a man sees that a 'breath of Will blows through the universe eternally in the direction of the right or necessary,' and 'throws him on the party of the Eternal.' Though 'This will derives from the aboriginal Nature, is perception of the Eternal Necessity . . . It is born, freedom, in the intellect.' Freedom is union in thought with the living whole. 'On that bright moment when we are born into thought, we are instan-

taneously uplifted out of the rank we had. Now we are of the
maker, not of the made.'

This flipping of the coin of necessity, revealing the source
of man's strength in the same terrific nature that makes him
powerless, lends a special quality to Emerson's acquiescence. It
is not a simple submission, but also a positive assertion of power.
Though his initial naïve egoism has disappeared, the pattern of
his original faith in man is transferred and adapted to the new
context. His view of human life remains dynamic and alive; his
thought moves still, with the vigor of practice, in the same pattern of organic polarity, from fate to freedom, from *outside* to
inside, as fact and mood demand.

The greatest man, theoretically, is still the hero or saint, the
man who, infused with the Will, possesses the secret of power.
Actually, however, Emerson's personal knowledge of power derives from the expansive moment of perception, when, by some
new awakening of thought from fact, he can experience afresh
his union with the Eternal. He could testify even in 1859 to
'The joy which will not let me sit in my chair, which brings me
bolt upright to my feet, and sends me striding around my room,
like a tiger in his cage, and I cannot have composure and concentration enough even to set down in English words the
thought which thrills me. . . . What if I never write a book or
a line? for a moment, the eyes of my eyes were opened, the
affirmative experience remains, and consoles through all suffering.'

Life continues to be an adventure, a challenge, and a promise.
Though men 'are miscellanies, rag-bags, unannealed glass, utter
discontinuity'; though the low and absurd predominates dis-
tressingly in our experience; yet great powers and influences clip
us round, and each moment is rich in hope. The old emotional
pattern of his inner life also persists into his later years——the
moment of kindling enthusiasm, as he glimpses 'the profoundly
secret pass that leads from Fate to Freedom,' and the ever longer
period of patient waiting afterward. Even in his habitual poverty, the old scholar can study, with some profit, the art of moral

and practical navigation; he can plot the spiritual condition of man in his era; he can take notes, not too hopefully, for a natural history of the intellect, 'a Farmer's Almanac of the mental moods, that I may farm my mind.' And from time to time a gleam from the interior depths will irradiate his superficial activity and recall him once more to his radical identity with the maker. Little wonder if his philosophy was optimism! 'What room for Fourier phalanxes, for large and remote schemes of happiness, when I may be in any moment surprised by contentment?' Such a man hardly dwelt, as has been argued, in a 'paradise under the shadow of swords.'

Yet his later thought does come closer than his first enthusiasm to the humanistic tradition which that Miltonic phrase, with its implication of a two-valued world, serves to characterize. Where in his early thought he suggests Thoreau, who sought a union with Reality through an immersion in wild nature, in his later he is more like Alcott, who felt that the best thing about nature was her susceptibility to human cultivation.

This transition to humanism was never complete or unequivocal. Yet that it did occur is demonstrated by that most humanistic of his books, *The Conduct of Life,* the finest product of his later thought. Begun as a series of lectures in 1851, it was revised and added to during that entire decade, being finally published in 1860. It is thus a distillation of the last decade of his intellectual prime, before the Civil War wrote its red Finis to his era, if not to his utterance. *Society and Solitude,* still excellent in its own way, is yet throughout on a slighter scale, as if the author felt that his real work was over.

The humanistic tendency of his thought during this last decade is indicated even in the title of his book. His general purpose, as he states at the opening of his first essay, is to study his own time. But he concedes at once, 'We are incompetent to solve the times.' A general theory of life is out of the question; man, immersed in nature, cannot command sufficient perspective to span the huge orbits of the prevailing ideas. But he can chart his relative position—orient himself, that is, for practical purposes. 'To me . . . the question of the times resolved itself into a practical question of the conduct of life. How shall I live?'

To this question Emerson now recognizes several possible answers. There are the two extremes, the transcendental concentration on power and neglect of fate, with its instruction to be great and ignore limitation; and the opposite fatalism, the too much contemplation of limits, which induces meanness. The fruitful and the human answer, Emerson now feels, lies in between, in a certain acrobatic balance, 'as the equestrians in the circus throw themselves nimbly from horse to horse, or plant one foot on the back of one and the other foot on the back of the other,' a practical reconciliation of theoretically irreconcilable opposites. We are subject to necessity; yet practically, a man must look on freedom, must act as if he were free, whatever the intellectual difficulties. Behind all lies fate, the law, to whose ordained order there is no exception; yet 'Forever wells up the impulse of choosing and acting,' which we cannot dishonor without violence to our nature.

By this somewhat Kantian road Emerson moves to an ethical position not far from that of the inventor of his literary form, Montaigne. He also is a kind of humanistic skeptic. He disclaims a capacity to solve the riddle of the age by reason; yet he also answers by implication the skeptical question, *Que sçais-je?*, with the affirmative answer, 'Enough to know how I shall live.' In ethics both are neither Stoic[1] nor skeptical, but humanist. Both even expound their humanistic ethics in an essay on experience; for Emerson's essay on that subject first and best formulated the ruling ethical point of view of *The Conduct of Life*. 'We live amid surfaces, and the true art of life is to skate well on them.'

To this skeptical empiricism Emerson adds, however, a third dimension, a sense of the relative depth or rank of various kinds

---

[1] In the sense, that is, of demanding of oneself an impossible greatness. Emerson's practical ethics retained a 'stern and exigent' Puritanical cast that was always considerably more Stoical than Montaigne's naturalistic virtue.

of experience which he called their *scale*. For the skating metaphor we should substitute the image of a ladder. The true art
of life, Emerson comes to believe, is to run well the scale of experience, to ascend without arrogance, and sink without skepticism. He could not, as he had once wished, ascend *and stay up;*
but the years in compensation did bring 'perspective so as to
rank [his] experiences and know what is eminent.'

As the metaphor of sleep and waking was the dominant one
in Emerson's transcendental years, so that of scale is dominant
in the later period. Whereas the force of the first was to oppose,
that of the second is to unify. The contradictions and anomalies
of his two-face experience are drawn together and given at least
the illusion of continuity by being pictured as two steps, however widely separated, on a common scale of values. Professors
Blair and Faust have argued that Emerson's essays typically
show a structure based on the twice-bisected line in Plato's
Republic. Though in their examples the parallel is not obvious
in detail, certainly these essays, and Emerson's later essays as a
regular thing, typically ascend *some* scale from lower to higher,
though the only points common to all scales, perhaps, are the
extremes which the scale serves to connect. The image expressed
and strongly supported his later mood of affirmation; for, just
as the effort to transcend his lower self, and the second thought
that this was impossible, left him in a dissatisfied mood of
impotent rejection, so, when he had accepted his compound
nature, he was equally cheered and heartened by the thought
that his higher self could never be left behind. Then he could
relax in the consciousness, 'The surface is vexation, but the
serene lies underneath.'

The two great principles of his *scale* ethics were Proportion
and Ascension. A man must learn to 'give to every being and
thing in the Universe its just measure of importance,' an end to
be accomplished not so much by a wide experience of a variety of
things, though some experience is necessary, as by the habit of
comparing the depth of thought to which different objects
appeal. A sense of proportion protects a man's faith and tranquillity when beset by nothings; he knows that these things are

transient, and that a recurrent deeper experience lies beneath. But equally it protects him from transcendental extremism, for the lower end of the scale also must be given its just measure of importance. 'Wine and honey are good, but so are rice and meal.'

The reason why the poem 'Days,' written in 1851 or 1852, though single in statement, yet seems ambiguous in mood, as F. O. Matthiessen pointed out, is perhaps that, while explicitly reverting to Emerson's transcendental state of mind and expressing his still recurrent sense of guilt before the powers that be for his obscure failure to make good his morning wishes, yet the situation it describes is actually conceived under the influence of the antitranscendental idea of scale and manages to suggest his own reply to the transcendental poet's self-accusation. An endless file of days pass by the poet, watching from the pleasant haven of his pleached garden:

> To each they offer gifts after his will,
> Bread, kingdoms, stars, and sky that
>   holds them all.

Can we fail to feel the suggestion in this scale of gifts that *all* are component parts of a human life? A man is not called on to choose one, and let the others go; he should choose and enjoy them all in proportion. There will always be other days. Only in the later verses does the file of days become one decisive Day, and the poem pass from description into myth. This part also is true to his experience, but two kinds of experience are suggested in the same poem.

If a scale implies proportion, it also suggests ascension. The chief use of a ladder is to be climbed. This implication he appropriately stressed in his essay on Plato. 'All things are in a scale; and, begin where we will, ascend and ascend. . . . All things mount and mount.' The great trick in life is to learn to ascend the ladder of things from the lower toward the higher. This ascension is now chiefly a matter of intellect. It is accomplished when we learn to see symbolically, to mount in the mind from appearance to Reality. Every man's consciousness is a sliding scale from deity to dust, from bread to sky. Let a man learn to use things, as far as his circumstances will allow, as steps on this scale and ascend as much as he may to an awareness of the enclosing ideal, and he will come as near liberation as the human condition will allow. There is also, Emerson never denies, a scale of power, with the moral sentiment at the top; but that is the way up for heroes; his way up is through thought.

The metaphor of a scale of ascension presides over *The Conduct of Life* in the form of Melioration, the idea of an ascending effort in man. On the surface an idea of progress, borrowing plausibility from the spiral tendency Emerson saw in nature, it is essentially a humanistic conception. Corresponding to the organic effort of nature to mount and meliorate is the impulse to the Better in the human being. The end of man is the development of character. Emerson's faith in his capacity for self-reliance has become a faith in his capacity for self-improvement. Fate and freedom still stand unreconciled in his thought, but the freedom now is not the ideal release of transcendental greatness, but the natural and relative power of choice of the humanist,—a freedom which, if it is a good deal less absolute than that claimed by the transcendentalist, yet has this advantage, that it exists.

The watchword of these essays is again Culture.[2] The task of culture, as he now understands it, is to refine and release the primary vigor of man. Every man has his proper bias, an original impulsion, by which nature contrives to get the work of the world done. A certain primary energy is the spring and motive force of life. The task of civilizing America, for example, was not the work of scholars, but of self-seeking, rough and ready, often evil men, who by sheer force did what had to be done. All vigor to live springs from this "original energy," without which manhood is impossible.

'. . . the end of culture is not to destroy this, God forbid! but to train away all impediment and mixture and leave nothing but pure power.' This it accomplishes by killing a man's exag-

2 See pp. 84-93.

geration. It removes his 'goitre of egotism' and brings him to society. 'Our student must have a style and determination, and be a master in his own specialty. But having this, he must put it behind him. He must have a catholicity, a power to see with a free and disengaged look every object.' 'Culture is the suggestion, from certain best thoughts, that a man has a range of affinities through which he can modulate the violence of any master-tones that have a droning preponderance in his scale, and succor him against himself.'

And how are we to get culture? To answer that question Emerson wrote his book. Culture, as always, lurks in all parts of life; anything may educate us, provided we are willing to learn from it. Look at the lesson concealed in the coarse matter of economy, the management of worldly possessions. One learns from it nothing less than the soul's economy, the chief principle of culture. 'It is to spend for power and not for pleasure. It is to invest income; that is to say, to take up particulars into generals; days into integral eras—literary, emotive, practical—of its life, and still to ascend in its investment.' 'The true thrift is always to spend on the higher plane; to invest and invest, with keener avarice, that he may spend in spiritual creation and not in augmenting animal existence.' So, as Emerson explores each of the leading topics of the time—success, property, education, religion, art—he is always on the lookout for what lessons each conceals for the conduct of life on every level. At the top are still the sublimities of solitude and heroism, but they are now only one element in a complex whole.

Like all humanisms, Emerson's ethics of culture is inherently patrician. It is an ethics for the superior man, the well-born soul. The necessary basis of culture now is the advantages of nature. There is a perceptible loss of interest in, though never a repudiation of, his first transcendental democracy, the potential greatness in every man; now his subject is aristocracy. To be sure, he means a Jeffersonian natural aristocracy, an aristocracy of character. But his book is not without class feeling. He is writing for and about the 'best people.' His topics are those that would naturally concern a prosperous middle-class group: Power, Wealth, Culture, Morals and Worship, Behavior, Art. The effect of his book is to take the usual concerns of the successful classes and translate them, by successive ascensions, into moral and personal terms. It is a gospel for gentlemen.

Through it one can see a certain change in his audience, above all in the Boston audience for whom he lectured most often, from a preponderance of the 'very quiet, plain, even obscure class, . . . young, or else mystical' who, he wrote to Carlyle in 1844, were the readers who belonged to him, to an increasing number of 'the great literary and fashionable army' who began in the next ten years to take him up. Never quite theirs, he adapted himself more than one might expect to their tone. Increasingly his companions became the solid and successful of the community, and less the young, or else mystical, for whom he was once the spokesman. The solitary *loco foco* who delighted Brownson in 1840 became the courteous and bland nucleus of the Saturday Club memorialized by Holmes. In the mirror of Emerson's thought, which is at the same time always distinctively his own and as responsive as a woman's to its surrounding atmosphere, we can watch his region modulate from its transient flirtation with transcendentalism to the genteel tradition. Progress replaces reform; culture, self-reliance; character, greatness. Brook Farm and State Street, reformer and conservative, youth and age are brought together in a common acknowledgment of a duty to invest their increasing incomes on the higher plane.

But Emerson always retained his dualism. Beyond his humanism lies his superhumanism. Life is a game which we play with what skill we can, but the wise man will see through the game and recognize the inventor, 'omnipresent without name.' Beyond the region of ethics and economy and the conduct of life, lies the lonely world of the one Life, the onward flow of the eternal Energy and the immutable laws it creates and obeys. The drama of human life is produced by the divine Life; human freedom is enclosed in fate. If one pole of interest in *The Conduct of Life* is the active, human one of virtue and culture, the other is the contemplative one of nature and necessity. This is the chief concern of the essays 'Fate,' 'Worship,' and 'Illusions.'

'Illusions' best expresses the feeling of this now habitual transfer of identity from the temporal to the ideal. It repeats once more the pattern of *Nature,* moving from idealism to spiritualism, though now the governing antitheses are those of his second essay on 'Nature': Motion and Rest. All things flow and change; that is to say, illusion is lord of this world. The thought is the same as that of his skeptical essays, and as with them the greatest spur to the sense of illusion is the thought of subjectiveness, the old secret suspicion that 'the play and play-ground of all this pompous history are radiations from your-self. . . .' The siren of 'the Berkleian philosophy' beckons him still from her bleak rocks—but now he presses on to a surer haven. The experience of illusion has been assimilated, as it had not been at the time of 'Experience.' Then he had the air of meeting an immovable fact with an irresistible faith, and some-how not quite observing the intellectual havoc that resulted. Now he has found that illusion too has its laws and limits.

For one thing, 'there is method in it, a fixed scale and rank above rank in the phantasms.' 'There are deceptions of the senses, deceptions of the passions, and the structural, beneficent illusions of sentiment and of the intellect.' The nebulous cloud of illusion is mapped and reduced to order. Furthermore, the greatest fear once engendered by illusion, the fear that man is an illusion himself, that all experiences leave us exactly where they find us, has been dissipated. Illusion instructs; 'our tuition is through emblems and indirections. . . .' If we wake from one dream into another dream, yet there is ascension in this suc-cession.

And above all, beyond motion lies rest. The capital facts of life may sometimes be hidden in the unpredictable play of our moods, but they are always there. 'A sudden rise in the road shows us the system of mountains, and all the summits, which have been just as near us all the year, but quite out of mind.' What then is revealed is the Law which rules the flowing. 'The

young mortal . . . fancies himself in a vast crowd which sways
this way and that and whose movement and doings he must
obey: he fancies himself poor, orphaned, insignificant. The mad
crowd drives hither and thither, now furiously commanding this
thing to be done, now that. . . . And when, by and by, for an
instant, the air clears and the cloud lifts a little, there are the
gods still sitting around him on their thrones,—they alone with
him alone.'

Law rules. The point is the same, for all the intervening
Oriental *Maya*, as that of his earliest reflections on his universe:
'virtue is the only lordship.'[3] So 'Worship,' in the manner of
'Compensation,' proclaims a faith in 'those simple and terrible
laws which, be they seen or unseen, pervade and govern.' From
the old conception of moral science he draws the old lessons:
that a man passes for what he is, that good is always rewarded
and bad punished, that an obedience to the moral perceptions
is the heart of worship. 'As we are, so we do; and as we do, so
is it done to us; we are the builders of our fortunes; cant and
lying and the attempt to secure a good which does not belong to
us, are, once for all, balked and vain.'

A worship of the Law remains Emerson's first stay and
foundation before the insoluble riddles of his existence. But if
the worship has remained unchanged, the worshiper has not.
Twenty-five years of reflection, since the provincial young Unitarian first set out to unlock the universe with the key of the
moral law, has left its legacy. What is man that he should pronounce on the nature of Reality?

> In many forms we try
> To utter God's infinity,
> But the boundless hath no form,
> And the Universal Friend
> Doth as far transcend
> An angel as a worm.

Was It even surely a Friend? The sense of a Power at the heart
of things to whom all man-made distinctions, even the distinc-

[3] See pp. 33-43.

tions of right and wrong, are an irrelevance, sent into his ideal
empyrean of love and virtue an occasional breath of 'murderous
cold' from remoter spaces where no faith could venture.

Then he sank to another sea, that of agnostic trust. All things
are alike saturated with deity. The secret will swallows up the
revealed will. The laws accomplish their inevitable ends by all
means. The living Heaven

> Sole and self-commanded works,
> Fears not undermining days,
> Grows by decays,
> And, by the famous might that lurks
> In reaction and recoil,
> Makes flame to freeze and ice to boil;
> Forging, through swart arms of Offence,
> The silver seat of Innocence.

By a surrender to destiny, in a blind confidence that it was
good, all shipwreck was made impossible.

This surrender is the upshot of his essay 'Fate,' his last serious
tilt with time and circumstance. He begins by asserting the two
contradictory facts. 'We have two things,—the circumstance,
and the life. Once we thought positive power was all. Now we
learn that negative power, or circumstance, is half.' 'This is true,
and that other is true. . . . What to do?' The solution of melioration is suggested, and given its due weight. The transcendental
solution of more power is stated, but the problem of achieving
power remains as dark as ever. The plain fact of moral freedom
is stated, to counterbalance the fact of necessity. But his final
solution is 'to rally on his relation to the Universe, which his
ruin benefits. Leaving the daemon who suffers, he is to take
sides with the Deity who secures universal benefit by his pain.'
The perfections of the Law that passes understanding make up
for all limitation in the individual. 'Let us build altars to the
Beautiful Necessity, which secures that all is made of one piece;
that plaintiff and defendant, friend and enemy, animal and
planet, food and eater are of one kind. . . . Why should we
fear to be crushed by savage elements, we who are made up of
the same elements? . . . Law rules throughout existence; a Law

which is not intelligent but intelligence;—not personal nor impersonal—it disdains words and passes understanding; it dissolves persons; it vivifies nature; yet solicits the pure in heart to draw on all its omnipotence.'

A necessitated freedom is thus the last lesson in *The Conduct of Life*. Law for man and law for thing are made of one piece; freedom lies only in obedience. 'And so I think that the last lesson of life, the choral song which rises from all elements and all angels, is a voluntary obedience, a necessitated freedom. Man is made of the same atoms as the world is, he shares the same impressions, predispositions and destiny. When his mind is illuminated, when his heart is kind, he throws himself joyfully into the sublime order, and does, with knowledge, what the stones do by structure.'

As the spirit of Emerson's rebellion can be summed up in his defiant claim, 'I am *Defeated* all the time; yet to Victory I am born,' so the spirit of his acquiescence is epitomized in a sentence from his second essay 'Nature': 'Let the victory fall where it will, we are on that side.'

CHAPTER TEN

Conclusion

AGE came gently to Emerson. At the age of sixty-one he noted in his journal, 'Within I do not find wrinkles and used heart, but unspent youth.' Yet he was aware of failing forces before the fact was plain to others and soon afterwards read to his startled son the beautiful poem 'Terminus,' in which he formally acknowledged, 'It is time to be old.' A clear sign of waning powers appeared at least five years before, when he wrote in his journal, 'I have now for more than a year, I believe, ceased to write in my Journal, in which I formerly wrote almost daily. I see few intellectual persons, and even those to no purpose, and sometimes believe that I have no new thoughts, and that my life is quite at an end.'

The crisis of the Civil War both arrested and insured his decline. The occasion was cunningly designed to tap the deepest reservoirs of his moral zeal. He had never, in his heart of hearts, accepted the duality of man; now he could participate in a crusade to cut the cancer of evil at least from the body politic. He still felt his uselessness as a scholar, scorned mere talkers, repined at the inaction thrust on him by his personal and human limitations; the furtherance of this holy war offered an unimpeachable practical use for his literary skills. He despised the shallowness of conventional success; 'the war searches character, and acquits those whom I acquit, whom life acquits, those whose reality and spontaneous honesty and singleness appear.' He resented the miasma of trivialities and illusions in which ordinary life was enveloped; before the strong wind of war, 'the whole drift and scud, with all its forms of bears, mountains, and dragons, vanishes out of sight, and the plain way of reason and right reappears once and forever.'

The battle fell on the land like the judgment of God. 'Let it search, let it grind, let it overturn,' he cried; and later: 'We

do not often have a moment of grandeur in these hurried, slip-
shod, aimless lives.' When the slaughter was over, he told a
Harvard assembly that the new era it had brought was 'worth
to the world the lives of all this generation of American men,
if they had been demanded.' Unlike Melville and Whitman,
younger and warmer men, he never 'felt the war,' as Hemingway would say. The fever of war-righteousness consumed his
last reserves of idealism; when its flare burnt out, he had nothing
left to say to the new age. The strongest refutation of those who
criticize Emerson for holding aloof from the practical problem
of realizing his ideals is provided by the spectacle of the waste
of quality when he finally did descend into the battle.

His creative life, in fact, survived the war for several years;
it was not until 1875 that Cabot was called in to help him
prepare from his manuscripts a new book for the press, though
his incapacity to do such work had been plain for some time.
Perhaps the date of another fire, the burning of his house in
1872, is best taken to mark the cessation of his inner life. Thereafter, with the progressive failure of his memory and power of
concentration, his hold on earth gradually relaxed, until we end
with the old man reading his own printed works like those of a
stranger—'and when his daughter came in, he looked up, smil-
ing, and said, "Why, these things are really very good." '

The life they recorded, the story these pages have had to tell,
is essentially a simple one. After Hume—to speak schematically
—destroyed his faith in historical Christianity, Coleridge supplied him a new object of faith in the Soul. The change meant
a loss of supernaturalism, a fusion of the divine and the natural.
Yet the profound distinction between the divine and the human
on which Calvinism was founded was not to be lightly superseded. Emerson continued to distinguish between 'experience'
and 'Reality' and interpreted his new faith to mean the revelation, in Coleridge's words, of 'another world indeed, but not
to come.' Accordingly, it seemed to him to guarantee the millennium and intoxicated his imagination with visions of an
imminent moral revolution. He entertained dreams of a Mes-

sianic greatness, when the Self would enter into its rightful
divinity and the huge world come round to him. This Saturnalia
of faith distinguishes his first years as a transcendentalist.

His millennial expectations, however, supported by little more
than theological habit, were soon undercut. Their intrinsic impossibility weighed them down and gave them a certain dream-
quality from the beginning. He thought his new faith clinched
the liberation toward which all Christendom had been working;
he learned that the God within had no power to affect his mortal
limitations. This realization was hastened by the radical egoism
that lurked in his hopes for greatness, giving them subversive
overtones even in his own mind which the reception of the
Divinity School *Address* did something to confirm; by what he
considered the futility of the reformers; and by his invincible
preference for a quiet scholar's life in which great action was
an intrusion. At the same time his conception of nature was
expanding and deepening in a way that made its dependence
on the self increasingly hard to accept. With time Emerson became sharply aware of the contrast between the transcendental
Self and the actual insignificant individual adrift on the stream
of time and circumstance. The Saturnalia of faith was offset
by skepticism.

Yet the eventual ascendency of experience over Reality in his
thought did not destroy his faith. That was founded on experience also, a direct experience of the God within, and could not
be shaken by contradictory facts. His growing naturalism, however, inclined him more and more to retreat from his first egoism
and to merge the self with nature. Then he reposed his faith on
the whole natural order of which man was an indivisible part.
His ethics of Self-reliance fell off to an ethics of vocation; he
replaced his hopes of performance with acquiescence and optimism. This shift freed his faith from the contradiction between
his belief in the possibilities of man and his perception of man's
limitations and allowed him to retain an agnostic confidence that
'Goodness is the only Reality.' His final optimism took him to a
wise and balanced empiricism, a detached report on the human
condition, and a genuinely humanist ethics. Yet it meant a defeat

of his first unworldly protest against the world, a defeat that laid a shadow of promise unfulfilled across his later serenity.

It is ironic and a little pathetic that so devoted a moralist and so honest a man should have drifted into a position which lays him open to the bad-tempered charge of Yvor Winters that 'at the core [he] is a fraud and a sentimentalist,' and which is leading increasing numbers of critics and readers to conclude that he is, in Eliot's phrase, 'already an encumbrance.' The logic of his faith forced him into a comprehensive acceptance that is more irritating than helpful in our disastrous times. In outline, the story of his thought seems an episode from a vanished past— his initial challenge a final eruption of protestant perfectionism thinly disguised as 'modern philosophy,' his eventual acquiescence close in spirit to what James called soft determinism; both now obsolete stages in an evolution of thought that seems unlikely ever to make them tenable again.

Yet the time and attention we still devote to him are not misplaced. We must be careful, as with any artist, to discriminate the quality of the man from his classification as a thinker. We must not, for example, overlook his unique sense of the practical and personal *immediacy* of ideas, what has been called his 'pragmatic mood,' because the ideas he chose as weapons are not those we would select; or contemn the spirit of high-minded rectitude in his life and writing because he found it easier than we do to hold that evil will bless—still less, because, to our discredit, we find his sense of duty distasteful; or close our minds, because of changing fashions of speech and opinion, to his memorable formulation of the individualistic principles that still must command our loyalty; or belittle the shrewdness of his *obiter dicta* on the American scene and the human condition because, to offset that condition, he took the road to an agnostic optimism. 'It is solely as character that he is important,' wrote John Jay Chapman, in his brilliant essay on Emerson. '. . . We must regard him and deal with him simply as a man.'

In the spirit of this quotation, my hope has been to bring to light the drama of the inner life that lay concealed, too successfully, behind the unruffled mien which he presented to the world. His life of thought was not, as it has generally been represented, an eventless and static thing, to be defined and assessed, like merchandise, by a process of random sampling. Apart from the question of their validity, his ideas have an intrinsic interest in their dynamic relations to each other. His thought has a personal if not a logical structure, a beginning, a middle, and an end. In following it we are watching a process that is always absorbing wherever it is encountered—the action of a superior imagination taking possession of its world.

It is only as we see him thus *sub specie temporis* that we can justly estimate his quality as a writer. His style has a surface formality, too, and also masks the fire under the Andes which drove him to self-expression. We are wrong to think of him as an Olympian seer, playing in solitude with Platonic abstractions. The power of his writing rests not simply on his craftsman's skill, though that was great, but on the compulsions and conflicts, the revelations and the doubts, the glories and the fears which struck fire in his imagination and compelled him to bring them to definition. Genius is the daughter of such necessity. Because he has this kind of power he will continue to be read.

Furthermore, it is not true that he has nothing to say to us. Emerson believed in the dignity of human life more unreservedly, almost, than any one who has ever written. Man possesses, he felt, an unlimited capacity for spiritual growth and is surrounded by influences that perpetually call on him for the best he has of insight and greatness and virtue and love. We think more meanly now, no doubt more truly, of ourselves and our world. But as long as we retain any self-respect, something in us must answer—whatever the second thoughts—to the faith in man that invigorates every page of these volumes. To reject Emerson utterly is to reject mankind.

Table of Abbreviations

W   *The Complete Works of Ralph Waldo Emerson* (Centenary Edition). Boston and New York, 1903. Vols. I-XII.

J   Emerson, Edward Waldo, and Forbes, Waldo Emerson (eds.). *Journals of Ralph Waldo Emerson*. Boston and New York, 1909. Vols. I-X.

L   Rusk, Ralph L. (ed.). *The Letters of Ralph Waldo Emerson*. New York, 1939. Vols. I-VI.

S   McGiffert, Arthur Cushman, Jr. (ed.). *Young Emerson Speaks*. Boston, 1938. A selection of sermons.

PH   Lecture course on *The Philosophy of History* (1836-37). Manuscript.

HC   Lecture course on *Human Culture* (1837-38). Manuscript.

HL   Lecture course on *Human Life* (1838-39). Manuscript.

ETE   Cameron, Kenneth W. *Emerson the Essayist*. Raleigh, N. C., 1945. Vols. I-II.

Life   Rusk, Ralph L. *The Life of Ralph Waldo Emerson*. New York, 1949.

Volumes are indicated by Roman numerals, pages by Arabic.

Appendix

NOTE A

ACCORDING to Stewart, writes Merrell R. Davis, 'the "moral sense" is a faculty having "active and moral powers" which influence the will of man. It has "pre-eminence" over all other principles of action, such as man's appetites, desires, affections, and self-love, and differs essentially from them in that the "least violation" of its authority "fills us with remorse." The moral sense is not merely the recipient of impressions of right and wrong, like the relishes and aversions of the external and internal senses, as Hutchinson had suggested, but an original and universal principle of the mind that apprehends the distinction between right and wrong to be "eternal and immutable." . . . These judgments spring from the "natural principles of the mind," which, like the "fundamental Laws of Belief," form an "essential part of the human constitution," and as such are "coëval with the first operations of the intellect." . . . Finally, . . . the moral sense enjoins upon us as the "law of our nature" the "love and admiration of moral excellence," and the exercise of its judgments is accompanied by the conviction of the moral administration of the universe and the belief in a future life.' ('Emerson's "Reason" and the Scottish Philosophers,' *New England Quarterly*, XVII [June 1944], 217-18.)

Emerson studied Stewart's *Elements of the Philosophy of the Human Mind* in college but would have found more information on this subject from the *Outlines of Moral Philosophy*, which he also consulted in his college years. In 1822 he read Stewart's *A General View of the Progress of Metaphysical, Ethical, and Political Philosophy* and recommended it to his friends; at about the same time he was referring in his journals to the earlier *Philosophical Essays*. Stewart stood high in his estimation in his early years as an authority on philosophical subjects and is a likely source for many of the ideas on other philosophers, like Berkeley and Cudworth, which Emerson has sometimes been assumed to have derived from the originals. (See Davis, and ETE by index; also J I 89, 287, 289, 298, 326; J II 25, 35, 133, 308, 329, 388, 435; L I 125, 132, 306; Cameron, *RWE's Reading* 46.)

Among other sources of this prevalent conception might be mentioned Price, Adam Smith, Butler, Cudworth, and such Realists among his Harvard teachers as Levi Hedge and Levi Frisbie. Price, of course, did not hold with a moral sense, but his ethical teaching reinforced the general idea for Emerson (see J I 78). Adam Smith's *Theory of Moral Sentiments* was in his hands in 1821, and again for three months in 1824 (ETE II 183). This is one obvious source for the term 'moral sentiment' that so often recurs in his later writing, replacing 'moral sense.' In several places he also echoes Smith's phrase 'the man within the breast' (see S 9, L I 174). His teacher, Frisbie, had written a review of this work (*Life* 81). He studied Butler's *Analogy* in class, and though there seems to be no record that he read the *Sermons,* the main source for Butler's criticism of the moral sense idea, it is plausible to suppose that he was at least familiar with Butler's argument. He had heard a good deal about Cudworth from Stewart and probably looked into the *Treatise Concerning Eternal and Immutable Morality* in college, though his enthusiasm for Cudworth's great work, *The True Intellectual System of the Universe,* appears to date from 1835 (see ETE I 57; but cf. W IV 294n, and J VII 95n). On Frisbie and Hedge, see Davis, and *Life* 81-82.

NOTE B

The Realists' position is most briefly summed up in Stewart's *Outlines of Moral Philosophy:*

According to the ancient theory of perception, sensible qualities are perceived by means of images or species propagated from external objects to the mind, by the organs of sense. These images (which since the time of Descartes have been commonly called *Ideas*) were supposed to be resemblances of the sensible qualities; and, like the impression of a seal on wax, to transmit their form without their matter. This hypothesis is now commonly distinguished by the title of the Ideal Theory.

On the principles of this theory, Berkeley demonstrated that the existence of matter is impossible: for, if we have no knowledge of anything which does not resemble our ideas or sensations, it follows that we have no knowledge of anything whose existence is independent of our perceptions.

If the Ideal Theory be admitted, the foregoing argument against the existence of matter is conclusive. . . .

Dr. Reid, who first called the Ideal Theory in question, offers no argument to prove that the material world exists; but considers our belief of it an ultimate fact in our nature. It rests on the same foundation with our belief of the reality of our sensations, which no man has disputed. (Paragraphs 19-22.)

Emerson's prose fragment entitled 'Ideal Theory,' dated by Rusk 1821 or 1822 (L VI 337-38), shows his early familiarity with this terminology:

It is an interesting inquiry, to examine our knowledge of material world. Doubts have been started which affect its existence.

In the first place what are the foundations of our belief of its existence. These are the evidence of our senses. . . . If therefore it be proved possible that the senses can be decieved [sic] your knowledge is entirely unsettled you have no further proof that what appears to exist does exist. . . .

I   Now that the senses may be entirely deceived or rather that they may not operate at all is evident from dreams. . . .

II   . . . It is manifest, then that we have no knowledge of the substances which affect the senses in any other manner than as they affect them. Therefore if it be possible to affect them in any other manner than by matter there is no need of the universe to account for our perceptions.

. . . Perhaps there are a multitude of minds in a corner of space deeming themselves surrounded with bodies and a vast universe which exist alone in their own imaginations. . . . if the delusion be perfect & consistent it may be delusion still.

It will be noticed that the young Emerson, if his argument derives from Stewart, apparently does not quite grasp Stewart's point. To him the Ideal Theory is not a theory of knowledge so much as a theory of the existence of the material world. In my discussion I use the phrase in his sense.

On the probable extent of Emerson's reading in Berkeley, see ETE II 163 and J VII 44. On this point I find myself in agreement with Mary Turpie, as against Cameron (ETE by index) and Rusk (L, *Life* by index).

NOTE C

The importance idealism assumed in Emerson's mature thought is familiar to every reader of *Nature*. His most treasured experiences became the delicious awakenings of the higher powers before which the world loses its solidity, until in his letter to Margaret Fuller he could write himself down flatly as an idealist. (See ETE, chapter on Berkeley.) At first a dream too wild, appropriate perhaps to learning's El Dorado, the Hindu mythologies, but hardly to a sober teacher of rational Christianity, this primeval theory gathers strength with his new faith, until, as *Walden* puts it, his bucket and that of the priest of Brahma and Vishnu and Indra grate together in the same well. This, he could feel, was the one solution to his nature and relations (W I 86, L I 117, L II 384-85).

Yet the theory retained its sceptical implications too, which gave him trouble when he was writing his first profession of faith, *Nature*, where he finally set it down as a useful introductory hypothesis. All depended on where the doubt of outward reality led. If it led, with the Ideal Theory, to doubt and illusion, then it must be resisted: 'It leaves God out of me' (W I 63). But if it led to, or sprang from, a strong feeling of the reality of things unseen (S 2), then it was beneficent, a sign of the awakened Soul. Yet we can see that even this highest idealism—what he preferred to call spiritualism—could not be embraced without reserve. A door to scepticism lay even at the gates of Jerusalem.

For one thing, 'the heart resists it, because it balks the affections in denying substantive being to men and women' (W I

63). Also, as he loftily remarked, 'so long as the active powers predominate over the reflective, we resist with indignation any hint that nature is more short-lived or mutable than spirit' (W I 48-49). In *Nature* he appears to believe that a perfect spiritualism will sweep away these objections. The whole record, as we will watch it develop, suggests rather that he never could reconcile the idealist's vision of the dance of the world, and his personal responsibilities in the conduct of life. 'When the mountains begin to look unreal, the soul is in a high state, yet in an action of justice or charity things look solid again' (J III 486). Idealism is scepticism still, a denial, as the Realists had taught him, of an ultimate fact in our nature.

Note D

As Parkes has remarked, Emerson's is in some respects one of the least modern minds among nineteenth-century thinkers. His exhilarating liberation, first from the paralyzing Calvinist belief in man's dependence on grace for salvation, and then from the almost equally paralyzing Unitarian belief in man's dependence for salvation on his own nearly unaided will and reason, served in the first instance only to release from its scholastic controls the primitive hunger for salvation at the heart of Puritanism. As a result, he tapped directly a wellspring of enthusiasm almost as old as Christianity. His contemporaries knew this and classified his 'latest form of infidelity' correctly as what the Puritans called Antinomianism. The affinity he felt for such an Antinomian group as the Quakers is well known, but parallels in his thought to other radical seventeenth-century sects are also visible, as to the Seekers or the Ranters, and parallels to enthusiastic Protestant splinter groups in his own day are equally striking. The Perfectionism of John Humphrey Noyes, in particular, almost deserves the name of Bible Transcendentalism. The millennialism, pantheism, and perfectionism, which in different degrees mark this kind of Christian enthusiasm wherever it has emerged, mark Emerson's enthusiastic philosophy also. For all the modern influences, without which, of course, his thought would never have grown the way it did, the result represents an emergence among the *clercs* of the anti- · clerical, enthusiastic spirit of popular infidelity, which then picks up as it goes its natural supports among the speculations of the scholars. Emerson, however, has nothing of the narrow fanatical spirit of most Protestant sectarians. Where they say *faith,* he says *reason;* where they say *grace,* he says *nature;* where· they say *true Christian,* he says *true man.* Between him and them has intervened the whole revolution of the Enlightenment. It brought him back to them in the end, in the manner this chapter has shown, but not without so transforming the assumptions underlying his new enthusiasm as to justify his conviction that the spirit of truth was speaking to him as it had never spoken to any previous generation. (See S 191-202. Consult also William R. Inge, *Christian Mysticism* [London, 1899]; Rufus M. Jones, *Studies in Mystical Religion* [London, 1909]; Elmer T. Clark, *The Small Sects in America* [Nashville, 1937]; Maurice W. Armstrong, 'Religious Enthusiasm and Separatism in Colonial New England,' *Harvard Theological Review,* XXXVIII [April 1945], 111-40; David M. Ludlum, *Social Ferment in Vermont, 1791-1850* [New York, 1939]; George W. Noyes, ed., *The Religious Experience of John Humphrey Noyes* [New York, 1923].)

NOTE E

By 1832 Emerson had read some Plato, notably the *Phaedo* and the *Apology,* but his intensive reading in Plato and Neo-Platonism appears to belong more to the later 1830's and after (Turpie). Among Christian mystics he knew chiefly Fox and the Quakers, with some reading in the Swedenborgians and a bit, perhaps, in Boehme. Though Coleridge was a main precipitant for his thought, his knowledge otherwise of what we might call Germanic mysticism was then very slight and never grew large (Wellek). His Oriental reading at this time was insignificant (Carpenter and Christy). A major influence, of course, was the Bible, particularly John and Paul. On the whole, one's impression is of a mind shaped primarily by the themes and doctrines of evangelical Protestant Christianity, with an overlay of training in eighteenth-century rationalism, and a smattering of reading, chiefly secondary, in the history of speculative thought —a mind which is then precipitated into originality (and further bolder reading) by contact with 'modern philosophy,' chiefly through Coleridge.

Bibliography

I list here some writings on Emerson, and a few on related subjects, which have influenced this book, together with certain recent items that seem to me important. The major primary sources on which this study is based are listed in the Table of Abbreviations. Further items affecting special points are listed in the headnotes for some chapters in the References.

Adams, James Truslow. 'Emerson Reread,' *Atlantic Monthly*, CXLVI (October 1930), 484-92.

Adkins, Nelson F. 'Emerson and the Bardic Tradition,' *PMLA*, LXIII (June 1948), 662-77.

Arnold, Matthew. 'Emerson,' *Discourses in America*. London, 1885. Pp. 138-207.

Baumgarten, Eduard. *Der Pragmatismus: R. W. Emerson, W. James, J. Dewey*. Frankfurt am Main, 1938. Pp. 3-96.

Beach, Joseph Warren. *The Concept of Nature in Nineteenth-Century English Poetry*. New York, 1936. Pp. 336-69.

Blair, Walter, and Faust, Clarence. 'Emerson's Literary Method,' *Modern Philology*, XLII (November 1944), 79-95.

Boynton, Percy H. 'Emerson in his Period,' *International Journal of Ethics*, XXXIX (January 1929), 177-89.

———. 'Emerson's Feeling Toward Reform,' *New Republic*, I (January 30, 1915), 16-18.

———. 'Emerson's Solitude,' *New Republic*, III (May 22, 1915), 68-70.

Brown, Stuart G. 'Emerson's Platonism,' *New England Quarterly*, XVIII (September 1945), 325-45.

Brownell, William C. 'Emerson,' *American Prose Masters*. New York, 1909. Pp. 133-204.

Cabot, James Elliott. *A Memoir of Ralph Waldo Emerson*. Boston and New York, 1887. Vols. I-II.

Cameron, Kenneth Walter. *Ralph Waldo Emerson's Reading*. . . . Raleigh, N. C., 1941.

Caponigri, A. Robert. 'Brownson and Emerson: Nature and History,' *New England Quarterly*, XVIII (September 1945), 368-90.

Carpenter, Frederick I. 'Introduction,' *Ralph Waldo Emerson: Representative Selections*. . . . ('American Writers Series.') New York, 1934. Pp. xi-xlviii.

————. *Emerson and Asia.* Cambridge, 1930.

Cassirer, Benjamin de. 'Emerson, Sceptic and Pessimist,' *The Critic,* XLII (May 1903), 437-40.

Chapman, John Jay. 'Emerson,' *Emerson and Other Essays.* New York, 1898. Pp. 3-108.

Charvat, William. 'American Romanticism and the Depression of 1837,' *Science and Society,* II (Winter 1937), 67-82. Cf. Mayberry, George. 'In Defense of Emerson,' *Science and Society,* II (Spring 1938), 257-59.

Christy, Arthur E. *The Orient in American Transcendentalism.* New York, 1932. Pp. 63-183.

Clark, Harry Hayden. 'Emerson and Science,' *Philological Quarterly,* X (July 1931), 225-60.

Commager, Henry S. *Theodore Parker.* Boston, 1936.

Dewey, John. 'Ralph Waldo Emerson,' *Characters and Events.* New York, 1929. I, 69-77.

Dugard, Marie M. *Ralph Waldo Emerson: Sa vie et son oeuvre.* Paris, 1907.

Elliott, George Roy. 'Emerson's "Grace" and "Self-Reliance,"' *Humanism and Imagination.* Chapel Hill, 1938. Pp. 148-68.

Emerson, Edward Waldo. *Emerson in Concord: A Memoir.* Boston and New York, 1890.

Firkins, Oscar W. *Ralph Waldo Emerson.* Boston, 1915.

Flanagan, John T. 'Emerson and Communism,' *New England Quarterly,* X (June 1937), 243-61. Cf. Smart, George K. 'A Note on "Emerson and Communism,"' *New England Quarterly,* X (December 1937), 772-73.

Foerster, Norman. 'Emerson,' *American Criticism.* Boston, 1928. Pp. 52-110.

————. 'Emerson,' *Nature in American Literature.* New York, 1923. Pp. 37-68.

Foster, Grace R. 'The Natural History of the Will,' *American Scholar,* XV (Summer 1946), 277-87.

Frothingham, Octavius Brooks. *Transcendentalism in New England.* New York, 1876.

Girard, William. *Du transcendentalisme considéré essentiellement dans sa définition et ses origines françaises.* University of California Publications in Modern Philology, IV, no. 3 (October 1916), 351-498. Cf. Sching, A. 'French Origins of American Transcendentalism,' *American Journal of Psychology,* XXIX (January 1918), 50-65.

Goddard, Harold Clarke. *Studies in New England Transcendentalism.* New York, 1908.

Gray, Henry David. *Emerson: A Statement of New England Tran-*

scendentalism as Expressed in the Philosophy of Its Chief Exponent. Stanford, 1917.

Harrison, John S. *The Teachers of Emerson.* New York, 1910.

Holmes, Oliver Wendell. *Ralph Waldo Emerson.* Boston, 1885.

Hopkins, Vivian C. 'Emerson and Cudworth: Plastic Nature and Transcendental Art,' *American Literature,* XXIII (1951), 80-98.

———. 'The Influence of Goethe on Emerson's Aesthetic Theory,' *Philological Quarterly,* XXVII (October 1948), 325-44.

———. *Spires of Form: A Study of Emerson's Aesthetic Theory.* Cambridge, 1951.

Hotson, Clarence Paul. 'Emerson and Swedenborg.' Unpublished thesis, Harvard University, 1929.

Howard, Besse D. 'The First French Estimate of Emerson,' *New England Quarterly,* X (September 1937), 447-63. [Comtesse d'Agoult.]

[James, Henry, Sr.] 'Mr. Emerson,' *The Literary Remains of the Late Henry James,* ed. William James. Boston, 1885. Pp. 293-302.

James, Henry, Jr. 'Emerson,' *Partial Portraits.* London and New York, 1888. Pp. 1-33.

Jorgenson, Chester E. 'Emerson's Paradise Under the Shadow of Swords,' *Philological Quarterly,* XI (July 1932), 274-92.

Kern, Alexander C. 'Emerson and Economics,' *New England Quarterly,* XIII (December 1940), 678-96.

Krutch, Joseph Wood. *Henry David Thoreau.* ('American Men of Letters Series.') New York, 1948.

Ladu, Arthur I. 'Emerson: Whig or Democrat,' *New England Quarterly,* XIII (September 1940), 419-41.

Lindeman, Eduard C. 'Emerson's Pragmatic Mood,' *American Scholar,* XVI (Winter 1946-47), 57-64.

Long, Haniel. *Walt Whitman and the Springs of Courage.* Santa Fe, N. M., 1938. See Allen, Gay Wilson. *Walt Whitman Handbook.* Chicago, 1946. Pp. 75-78.

Lovejoy, Arthur O. *Essays in the History of Ideas.* Baltimore, 1948

———. *The Great Chain of Being: A Study of the History of an Idea.* Cambridge, 1936.

——— 'The Meaning of Romanticism for the Historian of Ideas,' *Journal of the History of Ideas,* II (1941), 257-78.

Matthiessen, Francis O. *American Renaissance: Art and Expression in the Age of Emerson and Whitman.* New York, 1941.

McNulty, John Bard. 'Emerson's Friends and the Essay on Friendship,' *New England Quarterly,* XIX (September 1946), 390-94.

McQuiston, Raymer. *The Relation of Ralph Waldo Emerson to Public Affairs.* (Humanistic Studies, Vol. III, No. 1) Lawrence. Kansas, 1923.

Mead, George H. *Movements of Thought in the Nineteenth Century.* Chicago, 1936.

Michaud, Regis. *Autour d'Emerson.* Paris, 1924.

———. *L'esthétique d'Emerson: la nature, l'art, l'histoire.* Paris, 1927.

Miller, Perry G. E. 'Jonathan Edwards to Emerson,' *New England Quarterly,* XIII (December 1940), 589-617.

———. *The New England Mind: The Seventeenth Century.* New York, 1939.

———. *The Transcendentalists: An Anthology.* Cambridge, 1950.

Montégut, Émile. 'Du culte des Héros selon Emerson et Carlyle,' *Revue des Deux Mondes,* XX année, nouvelle période, tome VII (1 juillet 1850; supplément, 15 août 1850), 722-37. Cf. Cary, Elizabeth Luther. *Emerson, Poet and Thinker.* New York, 1904.

More, Paul Elmer. 'Emerson,' *Cambridge History of American Literature.* New York, 1917. I, 349-62.

———. 'The Influence of Emerson,' *Shelburne Essays, First Series.* New York and London, 1904. Pp. 71-84.

Mumford, Lewis. *The Golden Day.* New York, 1926. Pp. 94-106.

Parker, Theodore 'Theodore Parker's Experience as a Minister,' in *Life and Correspondence of Theodore Parker* by John Weiss. New York, 1863. II. 447-513.

Parkes, Henry Bamford. 'The Puritan Heresy,' 'Emerson,' *The Pragmatic Test.* San Francisco, 1941. Pp. 10-62.

Parrington, Vernon L. 'Ralph Waldo Emerson: Transcendental Critic,' *Main Currents of American Thought.* New York, 1927. II, 386-99.

Paul, Sherman. *Emerson's Angle of Vision: Man and Nature in American Experience.* Cambridge, 1952.

Perry, Bliss. *Emerson Today.* Princeton, 1931.

———. 'Emerson's Most Famous Speech,' 'Emerson's Savings Bank,' *The Praise of Folly and Other Papers.* Boston and New York, 1923. Pp. 81-129.

Royce, Josiah. *The Spirit of Modern Philosophy.* Boston and New York, 1892.

Sakmann, Paul. *Emerson's Geisteswelt.* Stuttgart, 1927.

Santayana, George. 'Emerson,' *Interpretations of Poetry and Religion.* New York, 1900. Pp. 217-33.

———. 'The Genteel Tradition in American Philosophy,' *Winds of Doctrine.* New York, 1913. Pp. 186-215.

Schneider, Herbert W. *A History of American Philosophy.* New York, 1946.

———. *The Puritan Mind.* New York, 1930

Schultz, Arthur R., and Pochmann, Henry A. 'George Ripley· Unitarian, Transcendentalist, or Infidel?' *American Literature,* XIV (March 1942), 1-19.

Scudder, Townsend *The Lonely Wayfaring Man: Emerson and Some Englishmen.* London and New York, 1936.

Seth, Andrew. *The Development From Kant to Hegel.* London and Edinburgh, 1882.

Shaw, Charles Gray. 'Emerson the Nihilist,' *International Journal of Ethics,* XXV (October 1914), 68-86.

Shepard, Odell. *Pedlar's Progress: The Life of Bronson Alcott.* Boston, 1937.

Sherman, Stuart. 'The Emersonian Liberation,' *Americans.* New York, 1922. Pp. 62-121.

Silver, Mildred. 'Emerson and the Idea of Progress,' *American Literature,* XII (March 1940), 1-19.

Smith, Henry Nash. 'Emerson's Problem of Vocation—A Note on "The American Scholar," ' *New England Quarterly,* XII (March 1939), 52-67.

[Spiller, Robert E.]. 'Ralph Waldo Emerson,' *Literary History of the United States,* ed. Spiller *et al.* New York, 1948. I, 358-87.

Thompson, Frank T. 'Emerson and Carlyle,' *Studies in Philology,* XXIV (July 1927), 438-53

——— 'Emerson's Indebtedness to Coleridge,' *Studies in Philology,* XXIII (January 1926), 55-76.

———. 'Emerson's Theory and Practice of Poetry,' *PMLA,* XLIII (December 1928), 1170-84.

Tolles, Frederick B. 'Emerson and Quakerism,' *American Literature,* X (May 1938), 142-65.

Turpie, Mary C. 'The Growth of Emerson's Thought.' Unpublished thesis, University of Minnesota, 1943.

Wahr, Fred B. *Emerson and Goethe.* Ann Arbor, 1915.

Wellek, René. 'Emerson and German Philosophy,' *New England Quarterly,* XVI (March 1943), 41-62.

———. 'The Minor Transcendentalists and German Philosophy,' *New England Quarterly,* XV (December 1942), 652-80.

Wells, Ronald V. *Three Christian Transcendentalists: James Marsh, Caleb Sprague Henry, Frederic Henry Hedge.* New York, 1943.

Whicher, George F. *Walden Revisited.* Chicago, 1945.

Whicher, Stephen E. 'The Lapse of Uriel.' Unpublished thesis, Harvard University, 1942. The first version of the present book.

Whitehead, Alfred North. *Adventures of Ideas.* New York, 1933.

————. *Science and the Modern World.* New York, 1925.

Winters, Yvor. 'Jones Very and R. W. Emerson: Aspects of New England Mysticism,' *In Defense of Reason.* New York, 1947. Pp. 262-82. Originally published in *Maule's Curse: Seven Studies in the History of American Obscurantism* (1938).

Woodberry, George Edward. *Ralph Waldo Emerson.* New York and London, 1907.

Young, Charles Lowell. *Emerson's Montaigne.* New York, 1941.

References

References are listed by chapter and page (in bold face type), in the order in which they occur, under the page on which each quotation *begins.* Short titles will be found expanded either in the general Bibliography or in the bibliographical note below. Abbreviations are explained in the Table of Abbreviations I have expanded abbreviations and added some punctuation in my quotations from manuscript sources (all of which are at the Houghton Library, Cambridge).

I include the date of each quotation, when ascertainable, in order to give a sense of the time-progression of my argument. Though to a certain extent this book describes the permanent structure of Emerson's ideas, I hope the general onward drift of the dates cited will help to show why I do not accept the possible contention that it does nothing else. At the same time particular cases in which I illustrate a 'late' idea with an early quotation, and *vice versa,* do not discredit my position, whose only adequate documentation is the whole body of Emerson's work.

Note: The following titles not in the Bibliography are referred to below: William Henry Channing, *The Life of William Ellery Channing, D D.* (Boston, 1880); William Ellery Channing, *The Works of William E. Channing, D.D.* (Boston, 1895); Emily Dickinson, *The Poems of Emily Dickinson,* Martha Dickinson Bianchi and Alfred Leete Hampson, eds. (Cent. Ed.; Boston, 1930); Ralph Waldo Emerson, ed., *Parnassus* (Boston, 1874); Edward Everett Hale, *Ralph Waldo Emerson* (Boston, 1902); James Russell Lowell, 'A Fable For Critics,' *The Writings of James Russell Lowell* (Riverside Ed.; Boston and New York, n.d.), Vol. X; F. O. Matthiessen, *The Achievement of T. S. Eliot* (Boston, 1935); Charles Eliot Norton, ed., *The Correspondence of Thomas Carlyle and Ralph Waldo Emerson* (Boston, 1883), Dugald Stewart, *A General View of the Progress of Metaphysical, Ethical, and Political Philosophy* (Boston, 1822); and *Philosophical Essays* (Philadelphia, 1811).

Preface

vii W I 76. W I 52; cf. W V 241, W VIII 20, X XII 277.

Chapter One

In addition to the titles listed in the Bibliography, the following have contributed to the present chapter: For the general religious background, Arthur C. McGiffert, Sr., *Protestant Thought Before Kant* (New York, 1929); Edward Caldwell Moore, *An Outline of the History of Christian Thought Since Kant* (New York, 1915); Richard H. Tawney, *Religion and the Rise of Capitalism* (New York, 1926); Thomas C. Hall, *The Religious Background of American Culture* (Boston, 1930); and Ernest S. Bates, *American Faith* (New York,

1940). (See also Appendix, Note D.) For the Puritan background, Perry Miller and Thomas H. Johnson, eds, *The Puritans* (New York, 1938), and Clarence H. Faust and Thomas H. Johnson, eds, *Jonathan Edwards: Representative Selections* (New York, 1935). For the evolution from Puritanism to Unitarianism to Transcendentalism, Olive M Griffiths, *Religion and Learning* (Cambridge, Eng, 1935); Frank Hugh Foster, *A Genetic History of New England Theology* (Chicago, 1907); Joseph Haroutunian, *Piety Versus Moralism* (New York, 1932); Sidney Earl Mead, *Nathaniel William Taylor* (Chicago, 1942), Herbert W. Schneider, 'The Intellectual Background of William Ellery Channing,' *Church History*, VII (March 1938), 3-23; George Willis Cooke, *Unitarianism In America* (Boston, 1902); Arthur I Ladu, 'Channing and Transcendentalism,' *American Literature*, XI (May 1939), 129-37; Clarence H. Faust, 'The Background of the Unitarian Opposition to Transcendentalism,' *Modern Philology*, XXXV (February 1938), 297-324; John White Chadwick, 'Channing, Emerson, and Parker,' *The Ethical Record*, IV (July 1903), 177-80; and Lenthiel H Downs, 'Emerson and Dr. Channing. Two Men From Boston,' *New England Quarterly*, XX (December 1947), 516-34. For the intellectual background, John Herman Randall, Jr, *The Making of the Modern Mind* (rev. ed; Boston and New York, 1940), Carl L. Becker, *The Heavenly City of the Eighteenth-Century Philosophers* (New Haven, 1932); Sir Leslie Stephen, *History of English Thought in the Eighteenth Century* (3rd ed; London, 1902); and Benjamin Rand, 'Philosophic Instruction at Harvard University from 1636 to 1906,' *Harvard Graduates Magazine*, XXXVII (1928-29), 29-47, 188-200, 296-311. I owe a point on page 20 to Mary C Turpie, 'A Quaker Source for Emerson's Sermon on the Lord's Supper,' *New England Quarterly*, XVII (March 1944), 95-101.

4 J I 292-93 (1823). Cf., on Emerson's early self-doubt, J I 137-39, 139-42, 234-37, 242-44, 267, 284-85, 345, 347, 360-67, 377-80; J II 36-38, 54-55, 111-13, 117-21, 135-37, 144-45, 148, 151, 162-63, 165-66, 179-81, 201, 227, 244-46, *et al.* J I 363, 367 (1824). 5 J I 365 (1824). W I 282 (1841). 7 Channing, *Works*, 233. 8 J I 361 (1824) J I 284 (1823) J IV 229-32, J I 78, J I 140. 9 J II 136 (1826). J II 137 (1826). 10 Hale 123. Cf., on Hume, J I 290, 292, 324-25, 359, J II 10, 77, 83-84, 121-22, 273-74, 325; S 125; L I 137-38, 140. L I 137-38 (1823). J I 292 (1823). 11 J II 83 (1826). J II 71 (1826). J II 183 (1827). Channing, *Life*, 450; cf. Frothingham 123. 12 S 125 (1831); cf. J II 325. S 124 (1831). S 122 (1831); cf. J II 273, 487. L I 170 (1826). J II 84 (1826). 13 J I 378 (1824). J II 115 (1826). L I 170 (1826); cf. J II 111. J I 301-2 (1823). 14 J I 164 (1822). J I 210-11 (1823). J I 325 (1823). 15 J II 77 (1828). Stewart, *View*, Part II, 172-73, 271. Hale 122 (1821). J II 101, 105 (1826); cf. J I 109, L I 214. L II 385 (1841). 16 W I 47 (1836). J II 77 (1826). W I 58 (1836). Stewart, *Essays*, 131. S 2 (1826). 17 J II 250 (1828). L I 174 (1826). 18 L I 174. J II 168, 166 (1827); cf. J II 117-20, 214, L I 195. 19 J II 222 (1827). L I 251 (1828). S 4 (1826). J II 222-25 (1827). J II 273, 111, 170. 20 J II 242 (1828). J II 298 (1830). S 200 (1833). S 199-200 (1833). 21 HC I 5 (1837). J III 235 (1835). J II 317 (1830). J II 509 (1832). J III 235 (1835). 22 S 200 (1833). J II 294-95 (1830).

J II 358-59 (1831)   Parkes 34. **23** S 203 (1833). Parkes 34 J III
209 (1833). **24** J II 395-97 (1831), cf ETE I 175-77.

Chapter Two

27 Norton I 160 (1838). J II 518 (1832). **28** E. W. Emerson 48
(1834). L I 435 (1835). *Life* 237-38. **29** ETE I 192 (1835). **30**
ETE I 191, 192, 193-94 (1835); cf. J III 235, 237-39, 272. **31** J IV
247-49 (1837). **32** Lowell 39. **33** J IV 128 (1836). J III 208-9
(1833). **34** J II 323 (1830), cf. J II 358, 404. W II 93. J I 96
(1822); cf. J II 389, J III 423. J II 140 (1826); cf. S 9-10, J II 160,
J III 423. **35** W II 102-3 (1839). W II 121 (1839). W II 107 (1837).
W II 116; cf. J IV .167. **36** W II 94 (1839). *Life* 111. W II 122;
cf.   J II 390-91, J V 175. W II 104   W II 120. **37** Schneider,
History, 247. J III 434 (1835). J II 250 (1828). W II 123. **38** W IX
83 (1834). J II 502-3 (1832). W II 120, 123. **39** E. W. Emerson
254 (1841). J IV 127 (1836). W I 40-41 (1835). W I 125 (1838).
40 W I 123-24 (1838). J III 555 (1835). Miller, *Mind,* 21. J II 445
(1832). W II 135. **41** W II 160 (1837). W II 275 (1834). **42** W
IX 207 (1863).   W I 119, 122, 120, 127, 125, 121 (1838). **43** W I
129, 133, 137, 133, 142, 147, 151 (1838). **44** W IX 63-64 (1845?).
45 W XII 413 (1839). W II 124-26 (1839). **46** J II 120 (1826).
W II 47. W III 48. Matthiessen, *Eliot,* 18. **47** W II 271-72. W I 338.
J IV 193 (1837). J IV 53 (1836). **48** W I 114-15 (1837).

Chapter Three

50 W II 44, 50, 61, 85, 63. W II 89 (1837). **51** W II 47. HC I 5
(1837). W III 77. W I 334 (1841). **52** W I 4; cf. J V 93. **53** J
IV 33 (1836). W I 49. **54** J IV 78 (1836). W I 76-77. **55** W I
71-72, 73-74, 73, 76. **56** Gray 9-10. **57** J IV 128 (1836). **58** J V
215 (1839). W II 51 (1839). *Song of Myself,* Sect 1. **59** J III 319
(1834). J III 285 (1834); cf. W II 74-75. J II 386 (1831). J IV 14
(1836). **60** J IV 243 (1837). J VI 110 (1841). PH XII 39 (1837).
61 J IV 241-43 (1837). HC I 18-23 (1837). **62** J V 411 (1840)
63 J IV 238 (1837). W VII 5. W II 213, 216. **64** W I 95 (1837).
W I 177 (1838). W III 83. **65** J IV 248-49 (1837); cf. W I 352.
W I 40. W I 106, 108 (1837). 'Fox' 3 (1835). W I 161 (1838).
W IV 7. **66** 'Luther' 28, 36 (1835). 'Fox' 13 (1835). W IX 32
(1841). W II 248. **67** HC IX 1-2 (1838). W II 250, 249 (1838).
68 W II 250, 252, 255 (1838). **69** W I 165 (1838), cf. HL II 31.
W I 99 (1837) W II 233. **70** W II 233-34. W I 20. **71** W I
221 (1841).

Chapter Four

A bibliography on Brook Farm appears in Lawrence S. Hall, *Hawthorne:
Critic of Society* (New Haven, 1944), pp. 191-93. On reform, see Gilbert V.
Seldes, *The Stammering Century* (New York, 1928), and Alice Felt Tyler,
Freedom's Ferment (Minneapolis, 1944), not overlooking her bibliography.
For the Swedenborgian background, see the numerous articles by Clarence P.
Hotson, as listed in Walter Fuller Taylor, *A History of American Letters*

(New York, 1936), p. 512; also Marguerite B. Block, *The New Church in the New World* (New York, 1932). I have also had the advantage of reading an unpublished paper on Emerson and science by H D. Piper.

72 W X 282 (1844). L I 405 (1834). J III 345 (1834). J III 557 (1835). **73** J III 374 (1834). L I 431 (1835). J III 424 (1834). J V 108-9 (1838). Cf., on Emerson's response to the attack on the Divinity School *Address,* J V 30-31, 36, 43-44, 75, 80-83, 91-92, 93-94, 100, 149-50; W XII 413-14; J V 177-79, 380-81. **74** W IX 13-14; cf. J VI 462. **76** W IX 133 (1842). J V 95-97 (1838). Cabot II 436-37 (1840); cf. L II 369, n. 479, W I 248. **77** W I 248-49 (1841). **78** L II 364 (1840). J V 473-74 (1840). Cabot II 438. J V 474 (1840) W I 276 (1841) J VI 316 (1842). W I 279 (1840). W I 276 (1841). W III 85. **79** W I 285, 283, 285, 286, 278 (1841). **80** W I 247 (1841). **81** W I 302-3 (1841). W I 299. J VI 294. J VII 222 (1846). **82** J V 469 (1840). W II 163. W II 161 (1839). J VII 81 (1845), cf. W III 73-74, J VII 250 **83** W I 99 (1837). W I 148 (1838). W III 89; cf. W III 113-14. W I 353 (1841). W II 161-62 (1839). **84** W I 354. HC I 6-7 (1837). J IV 340 (1837) J VII 98 (1845). **85** J III 211 (1833). W I 64. W I 175-76, 182 (1838). **86** W II 72. J III 472 (1835). L (unlocated). W X 208. HC I 25 (1837) Cabot II 735 (1838). Cabot II 743 (1840) W I 95. W I 10. **87** W I 11. J V 456 (1840). J VI 490 (1844) J III 227 (1833) **88** ETE I 231. L I 450-51 (1835) W IV 121. J V 510 (1841). **89** J III 297 (1834). PH II. **90** J III 293 (1834). 'The Naturalist' (1834). W III 14 (1840). Lecture on 'The Uses of Natural History' 65 (1833). J V 298 (1839). J VI 189 (1842). J III 292 (1834). **91** J VII 32 (1845). W III 194. W IV 121. W II 32 (1840); cf. W III 332. W IX 25 (1841). HL III 5 (1838). **92** W I 92-93 (1836). W II 214, 212 (1839). J IV 424-25 (1838). J III 285 (1834). PH X 11-12 (1837). **93** W III 196.

Chapter Five

94 W II 308, 318, 301 (1840). **95** J III 239-40, W IV 186. Emerson, *Parnassus,* 153. W II 306. J V 484 (1840). W VI 15. W II 318 (1840). **96** J V 484 (1840). W II 309. J V 477 (1840); cf. W II 69. W II 301, 307, 318, 319-20. **97** W II 308 (1839). W II 306. W II 307, 317 (1840). **98** J IV 444 (1838). W II 67. J IV 117 (1836). J V 518-19 (1841). Matthiessen, *Renaissance,* 62. **99** W IX 487 (1856); cf. J IX 27. J III 209 (1833); cf. J III 237-39. W VIII 296, 272-73, 276. **100** W VIII 279. J VII 98 (1845). W VIII 276 J VI 447 (1843) J VI 237 (1842). **101** HL VI 17, 25-26 (1839). W II 319 (1840). W I 168-69 (1838). W II 319. W VII 451 (1840); cf. J V 439. **102** W IX 19. H L VI 7, 8, 13, 16 (1839). **103** J IV 391 (1838). Carpenter, *Asia,* 82. W III 245 (1842). **104** J VII 520 (1848) W I 115, 354, W III 85. J VI 80-81 (1841). J VI 189 (1842). **105** J VI 189. W VI 234-35 (1851); cf. J VI 166, 214, 506, J VII 241-42. J VI 190 (1842).

Chapter Six

109 W IX 17. W IX 127 (1846). **110** W IX 40 (1837); cf. J IV 235-36, W IX 418. W I 76-77 (1836). **111** W III 83. **112** W IV 173, 186. W IV 160 (1845). **113** W IV 181, 151 (1845). **114** W IV 155-56. W II 62 (1837). W IV 159. Carlyle, *Sartor Resartus*, Bk. II, Chaps 7-9. **115** W IV 157. W IV 160-61 (1845). W IV 160. W II 272 (1837). W IV 177. W III 48, 50. W IV 178. **116** W III 45. W III 48-49 (1842). W IV 177, 178. J IV 316 (1837). W III 50 **117** W III 247 (1844). W III 50, 51-52, 52. J VII 296 (1847); cf W IV 174. **118** W III 59, 65-66. W IV 156. W III 59, 60. **119** W III 60, 59, 60. W III 64, 65 (1843). **120** W IV 183 (1846). W III 43 (my italics). **121** W I 63 (1836). W III 75-76, 77, 78, 81. **122** W III 76. *Stranger*, last chapter.

Chapter Seven

123 W IV 180, 184-86. **125** J III 298-99 (1834). **126** J II 445 (1832). HL VI 47, 49-50, 55-56 (1839). **127** J V 480 (1840). J V 313 (1839). **128** W II 140-41 (1837). J III 531 (1835). W I 195 (1841). W III 245 (1842). **129** J VI 482-83 (1843). W XII 87 (1846); cf. J VII 186. J VII 178 (1843). W III 284-85 (1842). **130** W III 242, 57. W III 184-85, 187 (1841). **131** W I 301 (1841). W IX 79. W IV 171, 170-71. **132** W III 193. W II 327. J VI 275 (1842). W II 325 (1841). **133** W I 10. J IV 12 (1836). J III 425 (1834). W II 274 (1838). **134** W II 69 (1838). J IV 315-16 (1837). **135** W XII 60-61. **136** Lecture on 'The Poet' 30, 21 (1841). W II 363 (1836). **137** 'Poet' 29 (1841). W III 7, 6, 8. W I 207 (1841). W III 5 **138** W IV 206 (1845). W III 42 (1843). W III 37. J V 327 (1839). J VIII 124 (1850). **139** J V 164 (1839). W I 371-72, 373 (1844).

Chapter Eight

141 Beach 331. J VI 497 (1844). J VII 81 (1845). **142** Carpenter, *Asia*, 13. W I 205 (1841). W III 195-96 (1840). W VIII 8 (1854). Beach 339. J VII 104 (1845). **143** W IX 55 (1841). Gray 40-41, 44. W I 202, 203 (1841). W VI 35. **144** W IX 181. W I 3. W I 34 (1835). W I 197 (1841). Beach 341. **145** W VIII 4-5, 8-9. J IV 130 (1836). J IV 354 (1837). **146** W III 179-80 (1844). W III 179. **147** W I 200 (1841). **148** Dickinson 116. **149** W I 99-100 (1837). W I 29 (1836). W II 85 (1835). J IV 331 (1837). W II 56 (1838). J VII 131 (1845); cf. W IV 46. **150** W VI 71 (1847). Beach 365. J VII 131 (1845). W II 293. W III 70. **151** Gray 47. W VIII 9. W IV 52. J VII 123 (1845). W III 236. W III 62 (1842). J V 526-27 (1841). **152** W IX 79. W IX 18-19. W IX 58-59 (1841). J V 268, 481 (1839-40).

Chapter Nine

154 E W. Emerson 254. Spiller I 383-86. **155** J VIII 406 (1853) J VIII 311, 312, 292, 291 (1852). J VIII 55 (1849). **156** J VIII 264

(1851). J VIII 78, 79 (1849). J IX 128-29 (1857). J IX 216-18
(1859). **157** J IX 221 (1859). J VIII 218-19 (1851).   J VIII 529
(1855). **158** J VIII 254 (1851). J VI 180 (1842). Jorgenson. W VI
4, 3. **159** W VI 3, 23. W VI 47 (1851). W VI 23. W III 59.
160 J VII 83 (1845). J VI 397 (1843). J IV 368-69 (1837). **161** J
VI 81 (1841) W IX 228 (1851). W IV 68-69. **162** W VI 166, 134.
163 W VI 134-35, 136-37. W VI 125-26 (1850). **164** Norton II 84
(1844). **165** W VI 318, 319, 318, 322. W VI 325 (1851). **166** W
VI 215. W VI 221 (1854). W IX 359 (1840). **167** W II 129 (1846).
W VI 15, 4. W VI 47 (1851). W VI 49; cf. J VIII 303-5. **168** W
VI 240. J VI 190 (1842). W III 195.

Chapter Ten

For background on Emerson and slavery, see Marjorie M. Moody, 'The
Evolution of Emerson as an Abolitionist,' *American Literature*, XVII (March
1945), 1-21. The recent article by Carl F. Strauch, 'The Date of Emerson's
Terminus,' *PMLA*, LXV (June 1950), 360-70, serves to remind one that
what I have called Emerson's acquiescence was not untroubled. He did not
achieve obliviousness but reached a settled pattern of consoling response to
trouble. See my article 'Emerson's Tragic Sense,' *The American Scholar*,
XXII (Summer 1953), 285-92.

169 J X 42 (1864). W IX 489-90. J IX 183 (1859). J IX 335-36
(1861). J IX 412, 429, 462 (1862). J IX 519 (1863). **170** W XI 345
(1865); cf. J X 105. W VIII v-xiii. J X 476. J III 371; cf. ETE I
187. **172** Winters, *Reason*, 279. Matthiessen, *Renaissance*, 193. Chapman 35-36.

Index

195

Gray, H. D , viii, 143, 151

Great Action, 37, 65-71, 79, 97, 129, 132. Cf. Greatness

Great Man, the, 65-69, 98, 104-5, 130, 157. Cf. Abstractionist, Actor, Conservative, Doer, Hero, Knower, Materialist, Observer, Poet, Reformer, Reporter, Representative Man, Saint, Sayer, Sceptic, Scholar, Skeptic, Student, Transcendentalist, Youth, Eloquence, Greatness, Temperament

Greatness, 4, 8, 40, 47-48, 51, 58-60, 65-71, 72, 79, 80, 103-5, 109, 117, 118, 125, 130, 148, 162, 163, 164. Cf. Action, Aristocracy, Character, Eloquence, Freedom, Genius, God Within, Great Action, Great Man, Heroism, Life (poetic), Man, Mastery, Millennialism, Poet, Power, Reform, Sovereignty, Transcendentalism, Victory, Will

Greaves, J. P., 81

Guilt See Sin

Harvard College, 6, 8, 135, 170, 176, Divinity School, 36

Hawthorne, Nathaniel, 3, 135

Health, 3, 18-19, 70, 85, 99-100. Cf. Vital Force

Hedge, F H., 56

Hedge, Levi, 176

Hegel, G W. F , 17

Hemingway, Ernest, 170

Herbert, George, 142

Herder, J. G von, 17

Hero, the, 65-69, 80, 134, 155, 157, 162, and saint, 67. Cf. Great Man

Heroism, 51, 65-69, 100, 132, 133, 163, and the Individual, 67, and virtue, 68, and prudence, 68-70 Cf. Greatness

Herschel, J. F W , 89

Hindus, 16, 153, 178.

History, 98. Cf. Christianity (historical)

Hobbes, Thomas, 14, 130

Holiness, 41, 59, 67, 68, 135, 149. Cf. Moral Sentiment, Virtue

Holmes, O W., Sr., 164

Humanism, 140, 156, 158-64 Cf. Culture, Freedom, Manners, Means, Self-Culture, Virtue

Humboldt, Alexander, Baron von, 89

Hume, David, 10-12, 15, 16, 53, 113, 170

Hunter, John, 142

Hutcheson, Francis, 14, 175

Hutton, James, 145

Idea, Platonic, 53, 65 Cf Platonism

'Ideal Theory, the,' 15, 53, 177-78 Cf. Idealism (Berkeleian), Realism

Idealism, 14, 15, 17, 30, 45-46, 53-54, 75, 92, 114, 120-22, 133, 136, 138, 141, 165, 178-79, Berkeleian, 9, 15-16, 53, 121, 165, German, 55, 141, 180, Oriental, 16, Platonic, 53, 55. Cf. Illusion, Solitude, 'Spiritualism,' Subjectiveness, Ideal Theory, Berkeley, 'Modern Philosophy,' Germany, Orientalism, Plato, Platonism

Identity. See Schelling

Illusion, 115-17, 121, 135-36, 165-66, 169, 178. Cf. Experience, Idealism, Skepticism

Immortality, 9, 11, 14, 15, 46

Impotence. See Powerlessness

Impulse. See Moods

Incapacity. See Powerlessness

Independence, 13-14, 17, 21, 25, 26, 27-28, 50, 51, 52, 56, 58, 62-65, 77-78, 86, 96, 155. Cf. Self-Reliance

Individual, Individuality, Individualism, 21, 30, 31, 47, 51, 54, 57, 60, 67, 102, 103, 122, 124, 128, 146, 150, 172. Cf. Self-Reliance, Temperament

Indra, 178

Infinite, 96. Cf. God

Inspiration, Instinct, Intuition, 18, 32, 48, 51, 56, 84-93, 99-100, 111-12, 135, 149, 157-58, 168. Cf. Freedom, Genius, God Within, Power, Reason, Sentiment, Surprise, Youth

Intellect, 79, 94, 126, 132, 136, 138, 144, 147, 156, 158, 161, 165, levity of, 117, 134-35. Cf. Reason

Invulnerability See Security

Jackson, Andrew, 140

Jacobi, F H., 17

James, William, 172

Janus, 30

Jefferson, Thomas, 163

Jesus See Christ

Johnson, Dr. Samuel, 32

Jouffroy, T. S , 17

Joyce, James, Finnegans Wake, 69

Kant, Immanuel, 17, 159

Kirby, William, and Spence, William, Introduction to Entomology, 89

Knower, the, 136, 137 Cf. Great Man

Lane, Charles, 81

Language of nature. See Nature (as revelation)

Laplace, Marquis de, 89

Lardner, Dionysius, The Cabinet Cyclopaedia, 89

Law, 33-46, 58, 124, 144-45, 148, 159, 165-68, and power, see Power (and law), moral, see Moral Law Cf. Acquiescence, Beneficence, Compensa-

Composition: Ruttle, Shaw & Wetherill, Inc.
Typographic Layout: Harry S. Rossiter
Printing: The Legal Intelligencer
Binding: John W. Clark's Sons, Inc.
Book Design: Gunther Wehrhan

CPSIA information can be obtained
at www.ICGtesting.com
Printed in the USA
LVHW020855191218
600901LV00002B/171/P